MW00532986

THE
LITTLE
BOOK
OF THE
WILD
ATLANTIC
WAY

HELEN LEE

The
History
Press

First published 2021
Reprinted 2021

The History Press
The Mill, Brimscombe Port
Stroud, Gloucestershire, GL5 2QG
www.thehistorypress.co.uk

British Library Cataloguing in Publication Data.
A catalogue record for this book is available from the British Library.

isbn 978 0 7509 9201 5

Typesetting and origination by Typo•glyphix
Printed by TJ Books Limited, Padstow, Cornwall

Trees for LYfe

CONTENTS

INTRODUCTION

From Victorian times, when Cornelius O'Brien had pavements laid along the Cliffs of Moher, and Charles Bianconi began operating charabancs from Galway to Clifden through Connemara, visitors and locals alike have flocked to the breathtaking scenery of Ireland's Atlantic coast. In 2014, Fáilte Ireland, the Irish Tourist Board, devised a marketing plan to encourage tourists to explore beyond the traditional stretches of coast such as Connemara and the Ring of Kerry, and to go off the beaten track, to lesser-visited headlands and harbours, promontories and peninsulas along the route they called the Wild Atlantic Way. Beginning at Kinsale in Co. Cork, where the Celtic Sea meets the Atlantic Ocean, this 2,600km signposted route, going south to north, passes through the counties of Cork, Kerry, Limerick, Clare, Galway, Mayo, Sligo, and Leitrim, finishing in Co. Donegal, at the village of Muff.

It is a coast of scenic contrasts. From the lofty cliffs of Slieve League in Donegal, to the shingle beaches of Connemara, the Atlantic Ocean crashes, or rolls gently, depending on the weather, onto the shores of Ireland. There is much to focus a camera on along the Wild Atlantic Way, with the changing weather making for a different photograph from one hour to the next. There are roaring seas, with white horse-capped waves crashing off headlands, or calm green, turquoise and blue waters lapping off sandy beaches. One minute the sun is glinting off blue water, and the next, the water reflects the greys of rain-laden clouds. On land, no two counties are the same. In Co. Clare, the white sandy beach of Lahinch climbs to the towering Cliffs of Moher. In Co. Sligo, Ben Bulben sweeps down to the sea, and between Co. Clare and Co. Kerry the waters of the Shannon river flow, through its estuary, to meet the waters of the Atlantic.

To our ancient ancestors, who stood on these shores in Neolithic times, it must have felt like they were standing on the edge of the world. They were the first of generations to leave their mark on this coastal landscape. The built heritage spans from Neolithic tombs at Carrowmore in Co. Sligo, to the twentieth century Galway Cathedral with its green copper dome. The ruined monasteries and castles, the colourful fishing villages and busy port towns, the decaying coastal defences and those sentinels of seafarers, the lighthouses, all have a history. The interactions of the people who lived, and still live here, have generated stories of wars, shipwrecks, heroic deeds and even a sea battle. For the thousands who emigrated from Ireland over the centuries, this coast was their last sight of Ireland. Some of those who left found fame and fortune, some who stayed contributed to the history of Ireland, and others who never ventured farther than their birthplace also had stories to tell.

The stories of the Wild Atlantic Way are made up of myths and legends, struggle and strife. It has inspired writers and artists, inventors and scientists. As long as the ocean continues to crash and caress, to ebb and flow along the Wild Atlantic Way, so too will history be made. It is a big journey for a little book. The chapters of this book follow a route from Co. Cork to Co. Donegal, looking at a miscellany of historical stories about events, people and monuments along the Wild Atlantic Way.

GEOGRAPHICAL INFORMATION

Length of the Wild Atlantic Way: 2,600km

Most northerly point: Malin Head, Co. Donegal

Most westerly point: Garraun Point on the Dingle Peninsula, Co. Kerry

Most southerly point: Brow Head on the Mizen Peninsula, Co. Cork

Highest point within 5km of the coast: Mount Brandon 953m Co. Kerry

Highest sea cliffs: Croaghan Sea Cliffs, Achill Island, Co. Mayo, at 688m

County with shortest coastline: Co. Leitrim, at 6km

County with the longest coast: Co. Donegal, at approximately 460km

The oldest rock: 1,750 million years ago the rocks at Annagh Head, Co. Mayo, were formed

Most-visited point on Wild Atlantic Way: Cliffs of Moher, Co. Clare, with 1.6 million visitors in 2019

The following timeline lists events and history that occurred within a 5km distance of the coast at points located along the Wild Atlantic Way.

1

A HISTORICAL TIMELINE OF THE WILD ATLANTIC WAY

4000–3000 BC   Neolithic man builds a cemetery of portal tombs at Carrowmore in Co. Sligo.

Circa 3200 BC   The cairn known as Queen Maeve's Tomb is constructed on top of Knocknarea in Co. Sligo.

3000 BC   Stone Age settlers clear trees from the coastal land of North Mayo. Using dry stone walls, they create a field system to farm the land. The Ceide Fields are discovered under bogland in the 1930s.

2500–1500 BC   Bocan Stone Circle is erected, possibly, as a sun temple, on the Inishowen Peninsula, Co. Donegal.

1700 BC   The Tuatha Dé Dannan, a tribe that invaded Ireland and saw off the first settlers, the Fir Bolg, make a settlement at the site of An Grianán of Aileach on the Inishowen Peninsula. In the fifth century, St Patrick christens the local chieftain, Eoghan. The Inishowen Peninsula is called after him. The restored stone ring fort at the site dates from the eighth or ninth century.

1100–800 BC   The remains of a youth, found buried at the stone circle at Drombeg, near Roscarbery Co. Cork, date from this period. One of the most impressive stone circles in Ireland, in

1923 archeologists discovered that it is aligned with the setting sun of the Winter Solstice. Also on the site is a fulacht fia, a trough used by ancients to cook food by filling it with water and heating the water with hot stones.

Circa 500 BC   The Celts and their influences come to Ireland. They speak Erse, the early version of the Irish language.

432   St Patrick begins his mission to convert the pagan Irish to Christianity.

441   St Patrick spends forty days fasting on the top of Croagh Patrick in Co. Mayo.

484   St Brendan is born in Co. Kerry. In the sixth century, he makes a voyage across the Atlantic Ocean and it is believed that he reached the American continent. He is known thereafter as St Brendan the Navigator.

534   St Sennan founds a monastery on Scattery Island, at the mouth of the Shannon.

560   The Battle of the Books in Co. Donegal.

600   St Fionán founds a monastic settlement on the larger of the two Skellig Rocks, off the coast of Co. Kerry. By the eleventh century, the monastery is dedicated to St Michael the Archangel. A community of contemplative monks build retaining walls to create flat terraces for their settlement of dry stone wall oratories and monastic cells. The monks carve and build 600 steps to reach the summit. It is thought that climate change, which resulted in colder, stormier winters, forced the monks to move from the island to Ballinskelligs on

the mainland sometime in the twelfth century. Skellig Michael becomes a Unesco World Heritage Site in 1996.

795   The Vikings attack the monasteries on the islands of Inishmurray in Co. Sligo, and Inishbofin in Co. Galway. In AD 824 they attack Skellig Michael.

904   The Vikings attack the ring fort of An Grianán of Aileach.

954   After numerous raids on Scattery Island, off the Co. Clare coast, the Vikings build a settlement and coexist with the monastic settlement.

1124   Turlough O'Connor, the King of Connacht, builds a settlement, known at Bun Gaillimhe, at the mouth of the Gaillimh river. The settlement later becomes the city of Galway.

Circa 1195   Corcomroe Abbey, in the heart of the Burren in Co. Clare, is founded by Donal Mór O'Brien, King of Thomond, for the Cistercian order. Dedicated to Sancta Maria de Petra Fertili or St Mary of the Fertile Rock, it is one of the oldest monasteries along the Wild Atlantic Way. The tomb of Conor O'Brien, grandson of Donal Mór King, killed in battle nearby in 1268, is one of the few surviving examples of a Gaelic lord's burial place.

1220   The Carmelites build an abbey on Clare Island in Clew Bay, Co. Mayo.

1232   Richard De Burgo is the first of the Anglo-Normans to come west of the River Shannon. He builds a castle at Bun Gaillimhe, which is destroyed by the O'Connors and the O'Flahertys. De Burgo retreats, returning in 1235 with reinforcements. He defeats O'Connor and begins building the walled town of Galway.

1245   Maurice Fitzgerald, Lord Chief Justice of Ireland, erects a castle, around which the town of Sligo is built. His castle is attacked and destroyed by the O'Connors.

1253   Thomas Fitzgerald, 1st Lord of Kerry, founds the Franciscan abbey of Ardfert.

1271   Richard de Burgo, grandson of the founder of Galway, Lord of Connacht, and 2nd Earl of Ulster, builds The Red Earl's Hall in the town. He is called the 'Red Earl' because of his ruddy complexion.

1305   Northburgh Castle, near Greencastle, in Co. Donegal, is built as an Ulster stronghold by Richard de Burgo, the Red Earl, who now has control of most of Connaught and West Ulster. In 1328, the Red Earl's grandson murders his cousin William in the castle, by slowly starving him to death. William's Connacht family retaliate and attack the castle in 1333. It brings an end to the power of the De Burgos in Ulster. The O'Donnells fill the vacuum.

1320   St Nicholas Church is built in the walled town of Galway.

1393   People living on a cliff edge are stranded and have to be winched to safety when a chunk of land breaks off from the coast, forming the sea stack at Downpatrick, Co. Mayo. It is known today as Dún Briste, the 'Broken Fort'.

1460   Rosserk Abbey, on the River Moy, is founded by the Joyce family for the Franciscan Order. They return to Co. Mayo, from where they were expelled in the thirteenth century. The abbey is destroyed in 1590 by the Governor of Connacht, Sir Richard Bingham.

1462   Moyne Abbey, like its neighbour Rosserk Abbey, is built on the banks of the Moy. Founded by the Blake family, it too is a Franciscan house and is shut down by Sir Richard Bingham in 1590.

1477   Christopher Columbus visits Galway and prays in St Nicholas's Church.

1484   King Richard III grants Galway a city charter. It is the only city on the Wild Atlantic Way.

1520   Dunguaire Castle, on the shores of Galway Bay, is built for the O'Heynes.

Circa 1530   Grace O'Malley, Pirate Queen of the West, is born.

1580   The Siege of Carrigfoyle Castle, on the Kerry side of the Shannon estuary, sees a garrison of Irish and Spanish defend the fifteenth-century O'Connor castle against an attack by Elizabethan forces, during the Desmond War. The gaping hole on the west side of the castle is caused by English bombardment with cannon fire, one of the earliest uses of cannon in Ireland. Some of the defenders are killed by the collapsing wall. Those who survive the siege are executed on Palm Sunday.

1588   King Philip II's Spanish Armada is defeated by the English navy in the English Channel. In September, twenty-six of the 130 ships of the Armada are wrecked along the Atlantic coast, between Donegal and Kerry.

1594   The Gaelic Lords of Ulster rebel against the English. It is the start of Nine Years' War.

1601   At the Battle of Kinsale, Elizabeth I's English army defeat a combined force of Irish lords and Spanish soldiers.

1602   Building starts on James Fort, overlooking the entrance to Kinsale harbour. It is named after King James I, Elizabeth I's successor.

1602   The March of O'Sullivan Beara. Donal Cam O'Sullivan Beara's participation at the Battle of Kinsale leads to an attack by the English on his stronghold at Dunboy, on the Beara Peninsula in Co. Cork. On 31 December 1602, he leads 1,000 of his clan on a fifteen-day march to safety in Co. Leitrim. They are pursued by the English army and they are attacked by Gaelic clans loyal to the Crown. They run short of food and, famously, kill their horses and use their skins to make boats to cross the River Shannon. Of the 1,000 that left Beara, only thirty-five O'Sullivans arrive in Leitrim, with only one of the many women surviving the epic march. Many die on the gruelling trek, while others abandon the march. O'Sullivan Beara flees to Madrid, where he is murdered, in 1613.

1607   The Earl of Tyrconnell, Rory O'Donnell, and the Earl of Tyrone, Hugh O'Neill, along with their families, leave Ireland from Rathmullan in Co. Donegal. Their departure for the Continent is forever known as 'the Flight of the Earls', and brings an end to Gaelic Ireland.

1611   Under the Plantation of Ulster, Sir Basil Brooke is granted lands in Donegal that formerly belonged to the O'Donnells. He refurbishes Donegal Castle in a Jacobean style and designs the town around a square, still known as The Diamond.

1631   Barbary pirates kidnap most of the townspeople of Baltimore, Co. Cork, carrying them off to Africa and selling them as slaves.

1636   The first written history of Ireland, *The Annals of the Four Masters*, is completed in Co. Leitrim.

1651   General Ludlow, a soldier in Cromwell's army, says of the Burren region of Co. Clare, 'there is not water enough to drown a man, wood enough to hang one, nor earth enough to bury him'.

1653   Cromwell's soldiers plunder Co. Mayo.

1680   Another fort, named after King Charles II, is built to defend Kinsale from possible French invasion. Charles Fort serves as a military barracks until 1922.

1689   On 12 March, the Catholic King James II arrives in Kinsale from France with 1,200 French soldiers and money to begin his campaign to retrieve the English throne, which he has lost to his Protestant daughter and son-in-law, Mary II and William III. He captures James Fort and Charles Fort in Kinsale Harbour; however, Captain O'Driscoll surrenders James Fort to the attacking Williamites. James II leaves Ireland the following year after the Battle of the Boyne, fought on 12 July 1690, where he and his Catholic supporters are defeated. He never regains his throne.

1730   Richard Cassels, renowned German architect, is commissioned by the 1st Lord Altamont to extend Westport House in the same year that he builds St Johns Protestant Church in Sligo.

1755   Lisbon in Portugal is struck by an earthquake on 1 November. The resulting tsunami hits the Atlantic coast of Ireland and leads to the silting up of the estuary of the Argideen river at Timoleague, Co. Cork. It also damages the Spanish Arch in Galway, the harbour at Kinsale and floods the land bridge connecting Aughinish Island, in Co. Clare, to the main land. Scientists today believe that the earthquake measured between 8.5 and 9 on the Richter Scale.

1775   Daniel O'Connell is born at Carhan, just outside Cahersiveen, Co. Kerry, on 6 August.

1786   The Commissioner of Irish Lights is founded, under an act of the Irish Parliament entitled 'An Act for Promoting the Trade of Dublin, by rendering its Port and Harbour more commodious'. The organisation is still responsible for lighthouses around the Irish coast today.

1795   The village of Louisburgh, Co. Mayo, is founded by the 3rd Earl of Altamont as a planned village. It is named after Captain Henry Browne, an uncle of the Earl, who was involved in the Siege of Louisbourg, Cape Breton Island, Nova Scotia, in 1758, where the British defeated the French during the Seven Years' War.

1796   A fleet of French ships sails into Bantry Bay in December. Stormy weather prevents the French invading force from ever setting foot on Irish soil, much to the disappointment of Theobald Wolfe Tone, who is on board one of the ships.

1798   Known as 'The Year of the French', various attempts are made to land French soldiers in Ireland to help with a rebellion led by the United Irishmen.

1798   The Battle of Tory (sometimes Donegal) is the only sea battle to have been fought along the Irish Atlantic coast. It is the final chapter in an attempt by the French to invade Ireland.

1800   Blennerville Windmill, Co. Kerry, is built by Sir Rowland Blennerhassett. It is the only windmill along the Wild Atlantic Way.

1804   In response to the threat of French invasion, eighty-one signal towers are built around the Irish coast to communicate on shipping movements. Tall square towers, similar to medieval tower castles, with the distinguishing feature of larger windows, are constructed on high headlands. Semaphore signals, using flags and balls arranged on tall masts, and viewed through telescopes, are passed from station to station. They are abandoned in 1815 when the threat of

French invasion recedes after Napoleon is defeated at the Battle of Waterloo. Seven Heads Signal Tower in West Cork and the signal tower at Malin Head are just two of many that are still standing.

1809   Coast Guard stations are set up along the coast. Their original function was not as a life-saving service, but to collect taxes and pursue smugglers. Until 1822, the service was provided by the Royal Navy.

1811   On 4 December, HMS *Saldanha* sinks in a storm off the coast of Donegal attempting to return to anchorage at Lough Swilly. All 253 crew die, including Captain William Packenham, a brother-in-law of the Duke of Wellington. The only survivor is Packenham's parrot, identified by a silver collar inscribed with the ship's name it is wearing when found. The sinking leads to the building of Fanad Head lighthouse.

1817   Fanad Lighthouse, built by George Halpin, who designed more than fifty lighthouses around the Irish coast, is lit.

1822   Scottish architect Alexander Nimmo is appointed Engineer for the Western District of Ireland. He is responsible for building more than forty piers along the Atlantic coast. The village of Roundstone, Co. Galway, grows around Nimmo's pier.

1822   The Board of Customs takes charge of the Coast Guard stations. Their remit extends to confiscating illegal poteen stills.

1831   Tarbert Bridewell, Co. Kerry, which serves as a courthouse and a jail, is opened and used until 1945.

1832   A cholera epidemic that has swept through Europe kills more than 50,000 in Ireland. Sligo is badly hit by the disease, with 1,500 deaths.

1839   A hurricane hits Ireland on 6 January, the Feast of the Epiphany. The 'Night of the Big Wind' wreaks havoc along the Atlantic coast. A ship is sunk near Arranmore Island, Co. Donegal, another at Kilkee, Co. Clare, and twelve members of the Coast Guard are drowned near Roundstone, in Co. Galway. Statues on the outside of Galway's pro-cathedral are also damaged.

1841   John Holland, inventor of the submarine, is born in Liscannor, Co. Clare.

1845–49   The years of the Potato Famine bring death and devastation to the people of Ireland, particularly to those living in the counties along the western seaboard. The failure of the potato, the main subsistence crop, leads to the death of at least 1 million people, and a further 2 million emigrate.

1846   Tralee Ship Canal is opened, connecting the town with Tralee Bay on the Co. Kerry coast.

1847   At Altar, West Cork, rector William Allan Fisher pays the starving Catholic community to build a new Protestant church. To employ as many people as possible, no carts or horses are used to transport the materials to the church site. During Black '47 the population of Altar only fell from 370 to 343, bucking the trend of the region. An Teampall Bocht Church is still the only Protestant church in Ireland with an Irish name.

1847   James Hack Tuke (1819–96), a Quaker from York and the son of a tea and coffee merchant, visits the West of Ireland, at the height of the Famine. On Achill Island, Co. Mayo, he sees the seas teeming with fish, but is upset to learn that the starving people of the island have pawned their boats and fishing equipment to buy food. He organises funding for new boats and a fish market. His letters to the *London Times* newspaper, highlighting the plight of the Irish, leads to further fundraising for soup kitchens and other relief.

1849   James and Mary Ellis, Quakers from Bradford in the north of England, move to Connemara, intent on alleviating the distress caused by the famine. During the eight years they live at Letterfrack they build a dispensary, a school, a shop and a temperance hall. They drain 11,000 acres of land and plant trees. Mary Ellis is credited with introducing fuchsia shrubs to Connemara.

1858   A monument, paid by public subscription, is erected to the memory of local landlord Cornelius O'Brien, near the Cliffs of Moher.

1860   The first real-time weather observation in Ireland is transmitted from Valentia Island, Co. Kerry.

1866   The first transatlantic cable telegraph is sent, from Valencia Island to Canada.

1868   Countess Constance Markievicz (neé Gore Booth), of Lissadell House in Sligo, is born in London.

1868   John McBride, participant in the 1916 Easter Rising and husband of Maud Gonne, is born in Westport, Co. Mayo.

1877   Tom Crean, Antarctic explorer, is born in Annascaul, Co. Kerry.

1878   Galley Head Lighthouse is built in West Cork. It has the strongest beam of any lighthouse in Ireland, with a range of 30km (19 miles).

1881   James Tuke, who visited Ireland during the Famine, finds little has changed when he again visits Connemara. He sets up the Tuke Scheme, funded by Government and his business contacts. The scheme pays for entire families to emigrate to Canada and America. Journalists report that the scenes on Black Sod Point pier, Co. Mayo, are not as distressing as usual emigration scenes as on this occasion whole families are emigrating together. Between 1882 and 1884, the passage of almost 9,500 people on ships leaving from Blacksod Bay is funded by the Tuke Scheme.

1887   The West Clare Railway, linking Ennis with Kilrush, opens on 2 July. The journey of 43km takes three hours.

1890   Michael Collins, one of the signatories of the Anglo-Irish Treaty of 1921, is born at Woodfield near Clonakilty, in West Cork, on 16 October.

1891   Arthur Balfour, Chief Secretary of Ireland, travels to the West of Ireland to see for himself the level of poverty that still exists. Based on this visit, the 1891 Land Act sets up eighty-four Congested District Boards to fund the building of roads and piers, encourage new farming and fishing techniques, and invest in industries, such as lace and tweed manufacture. The Boards buy land, organising its distribution so that the 'congested' plots, which cannot sustain the families depending on them, are increased to more economically viable holdings.

1898   John Millington Synge (1871–1909) visits the Aran Islands for the first time. There he finds the inspiration he needs for his plays.

1901   A Marconi Radio Transmitting Station opens at Brow Head, on the Mizen Peninsula, Co. Cork.

1902   The Daniel O'Connell Memorial Church is consecrated in Caherciveen, Co. Kerry. It is the only church in Ireland dedicated to a layman. A corner stone of marble, laid in 1888, came from the Catacombs in Rome.

1904   The Fastnet Rock Lighthouse casts its first beam.

1905   Writer John Millington Synge is commissioned by the *Manchester Guardian* newspaper to report on the work of the Congested District Boards. He is accompanied by artist Jack Butler Yeats, who is to provide illustrations. Synge writes twelve articles and is paid £25, while Yeats provides fifteen drawings, and is paid more. They travel to Connemara and Achill Island, revealing a level of poverty in some areas little changed from the days of the Famine.

1907   The French ship *Leon XIII,* a fully rigged cargo ship, gets into difficulties when her rudder breaks in a storm on 2 October. She is bound for Limerick with a cargo of wheat and is blown past the mouth of the Shannon and on to rocks near Quilty, Co. Clare. Local fishermen take to their currachs and rescue thirteen of the twenty-two French crew, while the remainder are rescued by a naval ship. The fishermen receive awards from France and a payment of £6 each from a fundraiser that saw money donated from all over Britain and Ireland. The bell of *Leon XIII* can be seen in front of the altar of the local Catholic church, Stella Maris, which is consecrated in 1911.

1907   A Marconi Transatlantic Radio Station begins transmitting messages from Clifden, Co. Galway.

1908   On 22nd December, SS *Irada,* travelling from Galveston, Texas, to Liverpool with a cargo of cotton, hits rocks on Mizen Head. Some of the crew are saved by construction workers building the new signal station at Mizen head.

1909   The Signal Station is opened. Explosives are used to alert shipping to the dangerous coast during fog. In 1920, at the height of the War of Independence, the station is raided and explosives stolen.

1911   The artist Paul Henry (1876–1958) moves to Achill Island, Co. Mayo, and paints 'Launching the Currach', among many other works, inspired by the Atlantic coast.

1912   Bridget O'Driscoll, Annie Jane Jermyn and Mary Kelly buy tickets to emigrate to America, from Barry's Shipping Agency, Ballydehob, Co. Cork. They are booked to travel from Queenstown to New York on the maiden voyage of *Titanic.* All three women get into collapsible lifeboat D and survive the sinking.

1913   Plans to build a harbour and a terminus at Black Sod, Co. Mayo to cater for transatlantic passenger ships are drawn up. Boasting one of the best anchorages in Europe, with enough room for liners to turn safely, it is deemed preferable to Galway. Passengers will board a train at Euston Station in London, travel to Holyhead, and cross the Irish Sea to Dublin, where a train will carry them to Black Sod. The First World War intervenes and the project never comes to fruition.

1914   The Grand Fleet of the Royal Navy docks in Lough Swilly, Co. Donegal.

1915   In May, *Lusitania* is torpedoed off the Old Head of Kinsale.

1916   On Good Friday, *Aud*, carrying weapons from Germany for the 1916 Easter Rising, is intercepted by the Royal Navy off the coast of Co. Kerry.

1919   Alcock and Brown make the first non-stop transatlantic crossing by air between America and Europe. They land near Clifden, Co. Galway.

1921   On the foundation of the Irish Free State, after almost 100 years in existence, the Coast Guard Service becomes the Coast Life Saving Service.

1929   Tomás Ó'Crohan's book *An tOileanach* (*The Islandman*), about his life living on the Blasket Islands off the Kerry coast, is published.

1931   The first radio beacon in Ireland is installed at Mizen Head signal station.

1933   Muiris Ó Súilleabháin, another Blasket islander, publishes his account of island life, in *Fiche Bliain ag Fás* (Twenty years a growing).

1935   A boat carrying islanders from Arranmore, off the Donegal coast, who are returning to the island from harvesting potatoes in Scotland, sinks with the loss of twenty people.

1936   *Peig: A sceal féin (Peig: her own story)* is published and becomes the best known of the Blasket Island books because a generation of Irish students study Peig for the Leaving Certificate.

1936   Black Head Lighthouse, on the south side of Galway Bay, is built to assist ocean liners making their way to Galway harbour. After the Second World War the ocean liner business does not return to Galway.

1937   The first aircraft operates out of Foynes Flying Boat Port, Co. Limerik on 25 February.

1938   Three Irish ports that are operated by the Royal Navy under the terms of the Anglo Irish Treaty are returned to the Irish Government by British Prime Minister, Neville Chamberlain. The three ports of Cork Harbour, Berehaven and Lough Swilly are known as 'The Treaty Ports'.

1939   The *Athenia,* a passenger ship, is torpedoed by a German submarine within twelve hours of the outbreak of the Second World War. Survivors are brought to Galway.

1939   On the afternoon of 4 October, a crew of Greek sailors come ashore at Ballymore, Co. Kerry. Their cargo ship, *Diamantis*, travelling from West Africa to England, with a cargo of iron ore, was torpedoed by a German U-boat off the Scilly Isles the day before. Although not obliged to, the U-boat captain, Commander Werner Lott, rescues all twenty-eight crew. He sets a course for the coast of neutral Ireland. In Dingle Bay, he releases the Greeks into a small lifeboat and waits to make sure they all reach Ballymore before heading back out into the Atlantic. Commander Lott is praised internationally for his compassion in saving the crew, although not in Germany. In 1984, he comes, to Co. Kerry, to meet some of the locals who helped the Greek sailors.

1940   Eighty-four Look Out Post (LOPs) and Eire navigational signs are constructed around the Irish coast. Those stationed at the LOPs record shipping and aircraft movements. The Eire signs and corresponding LOP number are made from whitewashed stones, and are visible from the air, indicating to airmen that they are flying over neutral territory. Allied airmen are later issued with a list of locations and corresponding numbers. The Eire sign at Malin Head, in Co. Donegal, is No. 80 and is one of a number that have been restored.

1941   An agreement between the Irish and British governments allows Allied planes to fly a path over the Irish Free State, which becomes known as the 'Donegal Corridor'.

1943   Daphne Du Maurier's novel *Hungry Hill* is published. It is based on the family of her friend, Christopher Puxley, who operated copper mines at Allihies on the Beara Peninsula, Co. Cork.

1944   Weather readings from Blacksod Point, Co. Mayo, play a pivotal role in deciding the date for the D-Day landings.

1948   The remains of William Butler Yeats are reinterred at Drumcliffe, Co. Sligo.

1953   The last twenty inhabitants of the Blasket Islands, Co. Kerry, are evacuated to live on the mainland.

1958   Peig Sayers dies in a nursing home in Tralee. She is buried at Dunquin on the Dingle Peninsula.

1963   Monsignor Hugh O'Flaherty, the Vatican Pimpernel, dies in Caherciveen, Co. Kerry.

1967   John Lennon, of The Beatles, buys Dorinish Island in Clew Bay, Co. Mayo, but he only visits twice and later sells it.

1969   Ireland's only cable car is opened, linking Dursey Island to the mainland of West Cork.

1971   The wreck of *La Trinidad Valencera*, one of the largest ships in the Spanish Armada, is discovered off the Donegal coast in Kinnagoe Bay.

1976   Liss Ard House, near Skibbereen, Co. Cork, is bought by Albert Bachmann, head of the Swiss Intelligence Service. The house will be a bolt hole for the Swiss government in the event of a Russian invasion of Switzerland. Renovations to the house include installing hi-tech surveillance equipment and enlarging the cellars, where the country's gold reserves could be stored. Switzerland is never invaded, and in the early 1980s when Swiss officials realise that they own the West Cork property it is put up for sale.

1977   On 26 June, British explorer Tim Severin reaches Newfoundland, having set sail from Brandon Creek more than a year earlier, on 17 May 1976. In a boat made from oak, covered in oxhide and propelled by oars and two goatskin sails, he and his crew of four prove that St Brendan the Navigator could have reached the New World in the sixth century.

1978   The fifth President of Ireland, Cearbhall Ó'Dálaigh, dies and is buried in Sneem, Co. Kerry.

1979   On 8 January, *Betelgeuse*, a French oil tanker, explodes while unloading its cargo at Whiddy Island in Bantry Bay. Fifty people die in the disaster, including seven locals working at the oil terminal.

1979   During the biennial Fastnet Yacht Race – from Cowes, around the Fastnet and back to Plymouth – 19 people die in a sudden storm that whipped up in the Atlantic.

1979   Lord Louis Mountbatten is murdered by the IRA at Mullaghmore, Co. Sligo.

1985   On 23 June, a bomb on board Air India Flight 182, travelling from Montreal to Delhi via London, explodes while in Irish airspace, killing all 329 passengers and crew on board. A memorial is later erected at Ahakista on the Sheep's Head Peninsula.

1986   *Kowloon Bridge*, carrying a cargo of 160,000 tons of iron ore pellets, runs into difficulty off The Stags near Baltimore, Co. Cork, on 24 November. All twenty-eight crew are rescued, but attempts to keep the ship afloat fail. On 3 December, she breaks in two and sinks, along with her cargo. Two thousand tons of diesel leak into the sea, killing marine life, birds and seals, and polluting the beaches of West Cork. Today the *Kowloon Bridge* is the largest wreck on the Atlanric coast accessible to divers.

1997   All lighthouses in Ireland are finally automated and there are no longer any lighthouse keepers.

1997   The National Famine Monument is unveiled by President Mary Robinson, at Murrisk, at the foot of Croagh Patrick, and on the shores of Clew Bay, Co. Mayo, commemorating 150 years since the darkest days of the Potato Famine in 1847.

2014   The Wild Atlantic Way is created.

2

COUNTY CORK

KINSALE: THE BATTLE OF KINSALE

The town of Kinsale, at the mouth of the Bandon River, boasts a natural harbour where Vikings took shelter from the Atlantic and which was, from the twelfth century, a thriving medieval town. Today this town of colourful waterfront buildings is a small port with a busy marina, and is regarded as the gourmet capital of Ireland. Here, the historic journey of Ireland's Wild Atlantic Way begins with one of the shortest, yet one of the most significant, battles in Irish history. The Battle of Kinsale, fought between the Gaelic Irish lords and the forces of Elizabeth I, was a long time brewing.

One of the seminal events in the history of Ireland was the arrival of Henry II, King of England and the Anglo-Normans, in 1171. He declared himself Lord of Ireland, granting territories to various Anglo-Norman lords. In the centuries that followed, attempts to anglicise the Irish were in vain, with many of the English lords going 'native' and resulting in them becoming 'more Irish than the Irish themselves'. One area, in the east of Ireland around Dublin and south to Kilkenny, did adopt English ways, but everything beyond 'the Pale', as the region was known, was Gaelic through and through. All along the Atlantic seaboard and in the midlands, the Gaelic lords retained the culture that had begun with the arrival of the Celts from 500 BC. They spoke the Irish language and were governed by old Celtic Brehon laws.

All this changed in the sixteenth century with the arrival of the Tudors on the English throne. Henry VIII turned his attentions to Ireland, declaring himself King of Ireland in 1541. Under his policy of 'Surrender and Regrant', Gaelic lords and Old English lords who had gone 'native' surrendered their lands to the Crown and, on condition that they pledged allegiance to Henry VIII and recognised him as King of Ireland, the newly created earls were 'regranted' their land. Of the four old Celtic kingdoms of Ireland, the lords of Leinster, in the east, were predominantly compliant. They accepted the new English administration and became more anglicised. However, the lords of Munster, in the south, rebelled against attempts to introduce English governance and were defeated. By the late 1580s, most of the nobility of Connacht in the west had also been anglicised. That left just Ulster, in the north of Ireland, as the only remaining Gaelic stronghold of Ireland.

The two most powerful Gaelic families in Ulster were the O'Neills of Tyrone and the O'Donnells of Tyrconnell, present-day Co. Donegal. For centuries both families had vied with each other for power and territory in Ulster. However, the external threat of Elizabeth I and her plans for Ulster brought Hugh O'Neill, Earl of Tyrone, and Red Hugh O'Donnell together under the common cause of preserving Catholicism and the Gaelic ways of Ulster.

What ensued was the Nine Years' War. The Earl of Tyrone had once been a loyal servant of the Crown, but by 1594 he was orchestrating a war against it. The Irish excelled at ambush warfare and defeated the English a number of times, most notably at the Battle of Yellow Ford near Armagh in 1598, the most resounding victory the Irish ever had over

English forces. This success led to other Irish nobles supporting Tyrone and O'Donnell and the near-collapse of English rule in parts of Munster, Connacht and even Leinster. To combat the Irish successes, in a three-pronged attack Queen Elizabeth I dispatched Charles Blount, Lord Mountjoy, to Ireland as Lord Deputy, Sir George Carew to Munster and Sir Henry Docwra to Ulster. Mountjoy marched north, burning crops, killing livestock and destroying the dwellings of any Gaelic lord who supported Tyrone and O'Donnell, leaving thousands of people facing a winter without food and shelter. Carew, as President of Munster, punished Gaelic lords in the south and Docwra sailed into Lough Foyle with soldiers and equipment with which to build forts. The tide of the rebellion was turning against the Irish.

The Ulster lords turned to Spain for help against the English. It was hoped the Catholic Spaniards would rally behind the Irish rebellion against their old foe. King Philip III agreed to send forces but unfortunately the venture was beset with problems from the start. Don Juan de Águila, an experienced soldier having served in Flanders, was given the task of leading the Spanish expedition to invade Ireland. But first he had to be released from prison, where he was serving a sentence for fraud. He is often portrayed in Irish history as the fool who landed his army in the wrong part of Ireland, although history has redeemed him. De Áquila wanted to go to Killybegs, landing as close to the northern lords and their Ulster territories as possible; however, bad weather forced his ships ashore at Kinsale on 21 September 1601 with 3,000 soldiers onboard. He was more than aware that he was at the wrong end of the country. De Áquila managed to take the walled town of Kinsale but for the next 100 days was under siege from the English, with many of his soldiers dying from hunger and disease.

Meanwhile, word reached O'Neill and O'Donnell that the Spaniards had arrived. In October 1601 they made the long march south through enemy territory. O'Neill travelled south on the eastern side of Ireland and O'Donnell and his supporters marched through Roscommon, East Galway and over the Shannon. When O'Donnell and his men reached Munster, Sir George Carew gave chase. He lost track of them as the Donegal men trekked 64 km in the darkness of night over the Slieve Phelim mountains in Limerick and Tipperary, their passage made easier due to the marshy bogland being frozen.

By December 1601 the Ulster lords and 3,000 followers had reached the outskirts of Kinsale. There they were joined by 600 Spanish reinforcements who had arrived at Castlehaven, 50km west of Kinsale. Additional support came from local families, the O'Mahonys, O'Sullivans and McCarthys. The English army was now surrounded, as De Áquila's soldiers, who still held Kinsale, denied them access to the sea. The ensuing battle should have been a fait accompli for the Irish.

It was the decision of the impetuous O'Donnell that led to the dawn charge on Christmas Eve 1601 that got the Battle of Kinsale under way. The Irish, more used to ambush tactics, were not prepared for the structured attack by the English Cavalry. Within minutes the Irish were thrown into disarray and the battle was over in less than two hours. It is not known how many died. One claim that the English lost just one soldier is most likely false, as many English and Spanish soldiers starved and died of disease during the siege of Kinsale prior to the battle.

After the battle, the Spaniards were allowed to leave Kinsale and return home, ending any further attempts by Spain to invade the British Isles. The Battle of Kinsale was the final nail in the coffin of Gaelic Ireland. The English now had the upper hand. As with all good history, the story did not end there. Both O'Neill and O'Donnell escaped after the battle. This story concludes at the other end of the Wild Atlantic Way, on the Inishowen Peninsula in Co. Donegal, with the Flight of the Earls.

OLD HEAD OF KINSALE: THE SINKING OF THE *LUSITANIA*

On the afternoon of 7 May 1915 the people of Courtmacsherry were going about their business as normal. Anyone close to the shore might have noticed the silhouette of a large ship on the horizon, some 22 km away near the Old Head of Kinsale, and may have recognised her as RMS *Lusitania*. Launched from the John Brown Dockyard in Glasgow in 1906, the Cunard Line vessel had made many voyages across the Atlantic, winning the Blue Riband, the prize for the fastest crossing, on four occasions. On that day she was coming to the final leg of a voyage from New York to Liverpool. Suddenly a loud explosion was heard, causing people to rush into the street. On the horizon they could see smoke billowing from *Lusitania*.

Tom Keoghan, a coxswain with the Courtmacsherry lifeboat, was on duty that day. He watched as the stricken liner began to sink and immediately summoned the rest of the crew. They set out in their rowing boat and reached the site three hours later. However, as *Lusitania* had sunk in just eighteen minutes there was little they could do to help.

At the time, the First World War was raging on the battlefields of Flanders. In February 1915 Germany had declared that the waters around the British Isles were a war zone and that any ship, naval or merchant, was a target for the fleet of U-boats sent to disrupt shipping to Britain and Ireland. This was contrary to established maritime agreements of the day, which exempted ships such as *Lusitania* from attack. The day before *Lusitania* set sail for New York, the German Embassy there posted a warning in the *New York Times* informing passengers that ships flying under the British flag or the flag of her allies were considered targets in the war zone around the British Isles. The ship's captain, William Thomas Turner, was advised by the British Admiralty that on reaching the Irish coast he should avoid sailing near headlands, travel at top speed of 21 knots and follow a zig-zag course. These were all ploys to make the vessel less susceptible to a torpedo attack.

Unfortunately, foggy weather around the Irish coast that May morning meant that Captain Turner ignored the Admiralty advice. As he passed the Old Head of Kinsale, the ship cleared a fog bank and was travelling in a straight line at 18 knots. He had received a wireless message an hour earlier warning him of U-boat activity in the area. Commander Walther Schweiger, on *U-20*, spotted *Lusitania*, a far bigger prize than the two merchant cargo ships he had sunk in the English Channel the previous day. He gave the order to fire a torpedo into the side of the ship, which struck just below the bridge, causing a loud explosion. Then a second explosion rang out and the ship began to list. Of the 1,959 passengers and crew, 1,198 perished in the waters of the Atlantic, including ninety-four children

While most of the survivors were brought to Queenstown in Cork Harbour, some of the bodies were brought to Kinsale. The local coroner John J. Horgan was quick to call an inquest, which was held in the Old Market House in Kinsale. He requested the presence of Captain Turner, who had survived the tragedy. Horgan's verdict found that the deaths were caused by a crime contrary to international laws and conventions of all civilised nations. About half an hour after the inquest reached its verdict, the crown solicitor for Cork, Harry Wynn, arrived in Kinsale with an order from the Admiralty that no inquest was to be held until a formal inquiry was convened and advised that Captain Turner was not to engage in any proceedings in Kinsale.

The Germans later claimed that *Lusitania* was a legitimate target as she was carrying weapons and ammunition in her hold for use in the British war effort. One torpedo was fired, yet two explosions were heard. It was widely considered that the second blast was the combustion of a boiler, although there was also the suggestion that it was indeed ammunition exploding in the hold, something the British Government vehemently denied. A dive on the ship in 2008 searched the cargo hold and boxes marked as oysters, butter and cheese were found to contain bullets, shells, gunpowder and fuses.

The Old Head of Kinsale is the closest land point to where the wreck of *Lusitania* now rests, 19 km off the coast, in 90 metres of water.

CLONAKILTY: MICHAEL COLLINS

Michael Collins, one of the great patriots of early twentieth-century Ireland, was born in 1890 at Woodville near Clonakilty. In 1906 he moved to London to work in the Post Office, much to the relief of his mother, who was concerned about the Nationalist influences in West Cork. However, in London Collins immersed himself in the Irish community, most notably joining the Irish Republican Brotherhood (IRB) in 1909. In 1916 he returned to Ireland to avoid being conscripted into the British Army, but mainly to participate in a rumoured IRB rebellion. That took place at Easter 1916. Collins was in the thick of the Easter

Rising, stationed at the GPO as an aide-de-camp to Joseph Mary Plunkett, who had noticed his potential in Irish Volunteer training camps. After the Rising, Collins was imprisoned in Frongoch, North Wales, until December 1916.

In 1918 he won the South Cork seat in the General Election as a member of Sinn Féin. All seventy-three elected members of the party refused to take their seats in the House of Commons in Westminster and instead assembled, in January 1919, as the first Dáil Éireann. Collins was appointed as Minister of Finance to the Provisional Government elected by the Dáil. His boundless energy saw him negotiate a loan for the now-outlawed Provisional Government, assist in breaking Éamon de Valera out of Lincoln Gaol, and most significantly leading a military campaign against the British in Ireland. A group of trusted gunmen, directed by Collins, assassinated numerous British civil servants, police and army personnel throughout 1919 and 1920. To combat these attacks the British introduced a new force, unofficially known as the Black and Tans. The bloodiest day of what is known as the Irish War of Independence was 21 November 1920, when Collins ordered the assassination of fourteen British officers and that afternoon, in retaliation, the Black and Tans killed twelve people attending a Gaelic football match at Croke Park, a day forever known as Bloody Sunday.

When a truce was called in July 1921, it was Collins, among others, who was sent to London to negotiate a settlement with the British. He was one of the signatories of the Anglo-Irish Treaty in December 1921 that led to the partition of Ireland, setting up the independent Irish Free State and eventually leaving six counties in the north-east of Ireland under British governance. As he left the room, Lord Birkenhead, a co-signatory, commented that he had possibly just signed his political death warrant, to which Collins replied, 'I may have signed my actual death warrant.' Collins emerged as the leader of the Pro-Treaty side of the split that inevitably occurred, while de Valera led the Anti-Treatyists. Civil war tore the country asunder in 1922.

On 22 August 1922, Collins was on a tour of West Cork travelling among his own people. He visited Roscarbery, where he met with family and friends and where he was allegedly told that he was in danger of an attack despite being in his home county. He chose to continue with his tour and at 8 p.m. that evening at Beal na mBláth his car was ambushed and he was killed. His prophecy had come to pass. When word spread of his death, Anti-Treaty prisoners being held in Kilmainham Gaol knelt and prayed for the repose of his soul. He was laid to rest in Glasnevin Cemetery, Dublin.

ROSCARBERY: JEREMIAH O'DONOVAN ROSSA

To the young Michael Collins growing up in West Cork, Jeremiah O'Donovan Rossa, from Skibbereen, would have been a childhood hero. The stories of how this Fenian was punished in British prisons would have fuelled his nationalist spirit. When the octogenarian O'Donovan Rossa (1831–1915) died he left instructions to be buried in the town of his birth, Roscarbery, West Cork. His funeral was to become the most famous thing about him, not because, contrary to his wishes, he was buried in Glasnevin Cemetery in Dublin, but because the oration delivered at his graveside by Padraig Pearse was the rallying cry to all Irish Nationalists, including Michael Collins, to join forces and rebel against British rule. Within a year the Easter Rising of 1916 had occurred.

O'Donovan Rossa was a teenager during the Famine years. It claimed the life of his father. His mother and the rest of his family emigrated to America, leaving him to be brought up by extended family in Skibbereen. The memories of those famine years prompted him to set up a secret society, the Phoenix National and Literary Society, where Irish independence was the main topic of debate. By 1858 he was sworn into the newly founded Irish Republican Brotherhood, a nationalist movement whose members became known as 'the Fenians'. O'Donovan Rossa was an active member, and in 1865 he was arrested and charged with high treason for planning a Fenian uprising. He was sentenced to penal servitude for life, but was released as part of an amnesty in 1871, which came about after an inquiry into the brutal way in which Fenian prisoners were treated. During his incarceration he famously threw the contents of his chamber pot over the Governor of Chatham Prison. As punishment he had his hands manacled behind his back for a month. A condition of his release meant he could not return to Ireland and in 1871 he went to America, joining Clan na Gael, the American Fenian organisation that was committed to the overthrow of British rule in Ireland. From New York he orchestrated a campaign of bombing attacks on British cities that led to him falling out with Clan na Gael. When he made a return journey to Ireland in 1894 he was greeted and feted by the IRB, who approved of his militant approach.

Jeremiah O'Donovan Rossa died on 29 June 1915 in New York. Tom Clarke, leader of the IRB, commented to his wife that O'Donovan Rossa could not have died at a better time for Ireland. The remains of the old Fenian were brought to Dublin, where thousands lined the streets as his cortège made its way to Glasnevin Cemetery. At the graveside, Padraig Pearse delivered an oration that became required reading in the school English curriculum in the late twentieth century. He called the English 'fools' for leaving Ireland her Fenian dead, and that 'Ireland unfree shall never be at peace'.

BALTIMORE: THE SACK OF BALTIMORE

In the thirteenth century the Gaelic O'Driscoll clan built a castle perched on a hill overlooking the coast in what is today the town of Baltimore. The castle, then known as Dún na Séad (Fort of the Jewels), was all that stood there for 300 years. In 1607 a group of English dissenters for whom the Reformation had not diverged enough from Catholicism, led by Thomas Crooke, arrived intending to settle in a remote area of West Cork and build a fishing community. Fineen O'Driscoll was glad of their arrival.

He had pledged allegiance to Queen Elizabeth I, who knighted him in recognition of his support. However, his son and heir (under English law) persuaded him to side with the Gaelic Lord of Ulster at the Battle of Kinsale in 1601. For this duplicity he should have lost his head but he somehow persuaded Queen Elizabeth to spare his life. While he was allowed to retain ownership of his lands, he lost much of his fortune in the failed rebellion and was in need of money. He was more than willing, therefore, to accept Thomas Crooke's offer to lease the land on the shore just below Dún na Séad.

A formal lease was signed between the two men on 20 June 1611, granting the land to the Dissenters for twenty years. Within ten years the village of Baltimore had been built and was a thriving fishing port where herring and pilchard, caught locally, were dried, salted and exported to Bristol. Baltimore was also a recognised haven for pirates who operated along the west coast of Ireland.

Leasing his shoreline to the Dissenters had not solved Sir Fineen's money troubles and he borrowed the considerable sum of £1,693 from his wealthier neighbour, Sir Walter Coppinger. When the time came to repay the loan, Sir Fineen did not have the funds and Sir Walter demanded ownership of Baltimore. In 1630, and before the affair was resolved, Sir Fineen died. Nonetheless, his case was brought before the courts, where it was decided that Sir Walter should take possession of Baltimore. He was anxious to evict the English Dissenters, whose lease was drawing to a close. However, the courts decided that since Crooke's community had brought wealth and prosperity to West Cork, they should be allowed to remain. On the night of 20 June 1631, the day their lease expired, the people of Baltimore slept in their cottages sound in the knowledge that their future was safe. Little did they know that their world was about to be torn apart.

That night, Baltimore was raided by the notorious corsair Morat Rais, a slave trader. In the 1600s, as well as the slave trade that saw Africans sold in their thousands as slaves to the West Indies and America, cities such as Algiers on the Barbary Coast had a thriving trade in European slaves. Corsairs were pirates, who in return for defending Algiers used it as a safe haven for their unsavoury slaving activities. Morat Rais was the Muslim name of Jan Jensen, a sailor originally from Haarlem in Holland who had settled in Algiers. With his knowledge of the North Atlantic, his raids for slaves brought him as far as Iceland. It was inevitable that he would eventually target Ireland.

For his raid on Ireland he left Algiers with two battleships carrying 280 Janissaries, an elite raiding army. Near the Cornish coast he attacked and sank an English ship captained by Edward Fawlett, capturing him and his crew of nine. Near Dungarvan he attacked two fishing boats, again capturing the crews but this time commandeering the boats.

The captain of one of these Dungarvan-based boats was John Hackett. It was Hackett who warned Morat Rais against attacking his intended target of Kinsale, advising him that there were too many English naval vessels in the port. Fawlett suggested raiding Baltimore instead.

The four ships anchored offshore and waited for nightfall before this motley crew of a Dutch captain, an English seafarer, an Irish fisherman and more than 200 Janisseries sneaked ashore. At 2 a.m. began what became known as the Sack of Baltimore. They began by burning the thatched roofs of the cottages lining the seashore, known as The Cove. The occupants were forced outside, where 100 people were seized and two men were killed for putting up resistance. While these captives were escorted to the waiting ships, the raiders turned their attention to the upper village. However, the shrieks and cries from The Cove had woken the upper village, where one villager began firing shots from a rifle while another began relentlessly banging a drum. The raiders, thinking that the army was on its way, took to their boats and fled.

They set sail, carrying off between 100 and 230 people. They were bound and held below deck on the journey to Algiers, where they were brought to the slave market. Men were sold into slavery, those with a trade such as carpentry making a higher price. Women were sold into harems and children were sold to work in families, who often treated them kindly and brought them up as Muslims.

Little is known of the fate of those carried away from Baltimore that night. For those left behind, they were traumatised by the raid. Fearful that the raiders would return, many villagers moved further inland towards Skibbereen. The pirates never did return and Sir Walter Coppinger got his wish, taking possession of the abandoned village. Was it a coincidence that the raid happened on the date that the lease signed by Thomas Crooke and Sir Fineen expired? Did Sir Walter have a hand in the attack? We will probably never know.

BROW HEAD: THE MOST SOUTHERLY POINT IN IRELAND

On Brow Head, the most southerly point of the Irish mainland, stands a ruin that could easily be mistaken for a derelict castle. The ruin is, in fact, a signal tower and one of eighty-one such structures built from Dublin southwards around the east, south, west and north coasts of Ireland. It is a reminder of the role played by the Atlantic coast in the development of telecommunications for seafarers.

In the eighteenth century, the nearby town of Crookhaven was a busy port, where it is said the harbour was often so full it could be crossed by walking across the decks of the docked ships. As the last harbour (or the first) for ships crossing between North Europe and America, it was the final chance for mariners to get provisions for their long journey, (or to replenish stores after weeks on the Atlantic).

Two attempted invasions of Ireland by the French in 1798 exposed how vulnerable the west coast was to invasion and attack. Signal towers were built on lonely headlands, approximately every 13.5km from each other. Beside each tower was a 15m mast with a crossbar. Flags and balls were arranged on this to signal a message, the recipients at the next tower using a telescope to read this and a codebook to decipher it. The signal tower operators were able to relay messages about shipping movements along the length of the Atlantic coast. The threat of French attack only receded after the defeat of Napoleon at the Battle of Waterloo in 1815, at which point most of the towers were abandoned.

The locations of signal towers were later used for other purposes. At Cape Clear, a lighthouse, the forerunner of the Fastnet, was built. Today, the signal tower at the Old Head of Kinsale is a *Lusitania* museum, but at Brow Head, by the end of the nineteenth century, it was once again used for communication purposes.

In 1895 Guglielmo Marconi, an Italian engineer (his mother was Irish), devised a way of sending a wireless message between two points. By 1901 he had built a wireless telegraph station at Poldhu in Cornwall and one at the site of the old signal tower on Brow Head. When he successfully relayed a message over 355 km between the two stations, his next project was a transatlantic transmission. By 1914 Marconi stations along the Atlantic coast, most notably at Clifden, Co. Galway, were communicating not only with land-based stations in North America but with ships at sea.

Marconi's technology was one of the factors that brought about the decline of Crosshaven as a haven port. Ships were safer and could travel further, the coasts were lit, and with wireless communication they were in touch with the shore and no longer alone in the middle of the ocean.

THE FASTNET ROCK

Travelling the coast near Mizen Head, the eye cannot help being drawn to the majestic lighthouse perched on the Fastnet Rock, some 16.5km out to sea. In Irish the Fastnet is called *An Carriag Aonair*, the Lonely Rock. Also known as the Teardrop of Ireland, this name evokes the emotions of many Irish emigrants for whom the Fastnet was the last part of Ireland they saw as they sailed west to North America.

The Fastnet is a jagged rock jutting out of the Atlantic and is closest to Cape Clear Island just 7km away. The first lighthouse on this coast was built in 1818, on the high headland of Cape Clear, beside the disused signal tower. However, Cape Clear was regularly shrouded in cloud, making it ineffective. After a shipping tragedy in 1847 when the passenger ship *Stephen Whitney* sank with a loss of ninety-two lives, the Board of Irish Lights decided that a new lighthouse was needed. The obvious location was the isolated Fastnet Rock, but could a lighthouse be built in such a hostile environment? The task fell to engineer George Halpin, who designed fifty-five lighthouses around the Irish coast during

his lifetime. The first lighthouse on the Fastnet Rock was lit and operational in 1854. Halpin appeared to have overcome the many challenges of building a rock lighthouse – however, it soon became apparent that the cast-iron structure might not withstand the ravages of the Atlantic Ocean. Lighthouse keepers reported regular, often significant, movement of the building. A cast iron casing was erected around the lighthouse in the 1860s. The lighthouse on Calf Island at the end of the Beara Peninsula, which was built in the same way, was blown away in a storm in 1881. The Board of Irish Lights was once again forced to review the structure on the Fastnet Rock and decided that a new sturdier lighthouse was needed.

William Douglass, who had experience of building rock lighthouses, was commissioned to design the new Fastnet Rock building. He planned a tapering tower built from granite quarried in Cornwall. At the quarry, each block was carved to dovetail with the surrounding blocks and each layer was laid out and numbered before being transported to Crookhaven. A steamer, the *Ierne*, was specially built to transport the blocks to the Fastnet Rock.

The first of 2,000 blocks was laid in 1899 and the process was overseen by master mason James Kavanagh, who remained on the Fastnet Rock for months at a time during construction. The 2,000 blocks were laid in eighty-nine courses, the first ten of which were built into the island's rock face. The joints between the blocks were sealed with molten lead. By May 1904 the second Fastnet lighthouse was casting its beam across the Atlantic to a distance of 27 nautical miles. The lamp was initially lit using vaporised paraffin oil but was converted to electricity in 1969. A team of six keepers operated the Fastnet Lighthouse, with four living in the lighthouse at a time, each staying for a month, with two weeks off. If the weather was bad they often had to remain longer. In 1989 the Fastnet Lighthouse was automated. The Lonely Rock was alone again.

Every two years the Fastnet Rock is the turning point for the eponymous yacht race. Leaving from Cowes on the Isle of Wight, the 950km race passes the Scilly Isles, rounds the Fastnet and returns to England. On 11 August 1979, 330 yachts of various sizes, operated by crews with varying levels of experience, set out from Cowes. Edward Heath, former British Prime Minister, was among those participating. The weather forecast was good – however, by Monday, 13 August, the sailors found themselves in the midst of hurricane-force winds and high seas. An unexpected summer storm had come in from the Atlantic. Some yachts were able to find shelter in ports and harbours along the south coast of Ireland but others were not so fortunate. The biggest search and rescue operation ever undertaken in peacetime went into action. The RAF and the Irish Navy along with RNLI boats from Baltimore and other Irish ports went to help the stricken sailors. The Irish continental ferry sailing from Rosslare to Le Havre diverted to help in the rescue attempt.

The lighthouse keepers of the Fastnet also played a part. Unable to physically go to the aid of yachts, they were at least able to record the mast numbers of boats that passed the lighthouse and relay the details to the emergency services. Of the 330 yachts that set out on the 1979 Fastnet Race, only eighty-six completed it. The crews of twenty-five yachts abandoned ship, five of which sank, and twenty-five people lost their lives. Following an enquiry, the organisers, the Royal Ocean Club, introduced new regulations for competitors. All yachts had to carry VHF radios, sailors had to have a certain number of hours at sea and in the event of stormy seas they were to remain with their yacht, as most of the fatalities had been in life rafts.

The sea is unpredictable and dangerous, but the Fastnet Lighthouse has stood tall and straight against its hazards for more than 100 years.

BANTRY BAY: THE FRENCH INVASION OF 1796

A young Trinity College student, Theobald Wolfe Tone, was among a group of men who founded the Society of the United Irishmen in Belfast in 1791. Disguised as a literary and debating society, their real purpose was to discuss the recent events in France. The French Revolution of 1789 led to the establishment of a French Republic: governance for the people by the people. The United Irishmen aimed to bring Irish men of every creed; Catholic, Anglican and Presbyterian together to fight for the common cause of establishing an Irish Republic and ousting the British from Ireland.

Events in France, particularly the execution of King Louis XVI and his queen, Marie Antoinette, in 1793 had alarmed the British establishment. The United Irishmen were outlawed for their seditious views, but people such as Lord Edward Fitzgerald and Wolfe Tone were not discouraged.

In 1796 Tone, who is regarded as the 'father of Irish Republicanism', travelled to France with the aim of persuading the French to send an army to Ireland, where they would be joined by the United Irishmen in a rebellion against British rule. While his actions were considered treasonable by many throughout Britain and Ireland, the French knew that aiding an Irish rebellion would be a blow to Great Britain.

On 15 December 1796, forty-three French ships carrying 14,500 soldiers sailed from Brest, bound for Ireland. Tone, on board the *Indomitable*, was full of hope that the largest ever invasion of Ireland and the combined efforts of the French and the United Irishmen would finally lead to the establishment of an Irish republic. The biggest threat to this success was the Royal Navy. Britannia ruled the waves, but by sailing for Ireland in December, when most Royal Navy ships would be at anchor in safe ports, it was hoped that Britainnia's rule would come to an end. Their destination was Bantry Bay where, once disembarked, the commander-in-chief of the expedition, General Lazare Hoche, planned to march on Cork city.

From the very beginning the expedition ran into problems. One ship, *Seduissant*, ran aground on rocks before even reaching open seas. Once out into the Atlantic the fleet became separated. By 21 December only thirty of the fleet's ships had reached the rendezvous point off the Fastnet Rock. However, there was no sign of *Fraternité*, the ship carrying General Hoche. In a diary entry on that date Tone wondered what they would do if, 'the General should not join us?' Unknown to him, weather had forced *Fraternité* to return to France and weather was what ultimately doomed the entire expedition. On 24 December the fleet decided it should make for Bantry Bay.

Meanwhile, on shore, the French ships had lost all element of surprise and word had reached Bantry that the French were coming. The main landowner, Richard White, sent a boat with ten locals on board to assess the number of ships. When they did not return, White sent word to the army garrison in Cork and began preparations for the defence of Bantry. When the army arrived he provided his house for their use. Not everyone in Ireland was behind the United Irishmen and many were fearful of the guillotine-happy French.

By now, a violent storm was battering the south-west coast. Sixteen French ships were blown into Bantry Bay and were buffeted about by the gale-force winds. Some managed to anchor in the bay, but their lines broke and they were swept out to sea with a change in the wind. Some came close to the shore but were unable to dock. Tone famously recorded in his diary that they were so close to land he could have tossed a biscuit ashore. By 26 December, the ships were heading back to France without one soldier having set foot on Irish soil. Those ships that survived the winter storm arrived back to France on 1 January without seeing a single Royal Naval ship. Another record in Tone's diary suggests that England had not had such a lucky escape since the Spanish Armada.

In March 1797 Richard White was raised to the peerage as Baron Bantry for having 'been the means for dispelling the French fleet'. While he had rallied the troops, it was undoubtedly the weather that had dispelled the French fleet.

This was not the end of the story. Wolfe Tone persuaded the French to come to Ireland again in 1798 in what became known as The Year of the French and which was played out on the coast of County Donegal.

GLENGARRIFF: GARINISH ISLAND'S SUBTROPICAL GARDEN

The island of Ilnacullin (Island of Holly) nestles in a sheltered inlet of Bantry Bay at Glengarriff. Today travellers on the Wild Atlantic Way can take a short boat trip to the island, certain of seeing grey seals lounging on the rocks as they go to visit the formal gardens that were created on this island as a labour of love in the early 1900s.

In 1800, Ilnacullin was a barren 15-hectare rock, where locals grazed cattle and cut turf, but where no one lived. In 1804, the British Ministry for War took possession of the island. Only eight years earlier the French had attempted an invasion through Bantry Bay and the British were concerned that their arch-enemy Napoleon might consider Bantry as a point of access to invade the British Isles. The first Martello tower built in Ireland was erected at the highest point on Ilnacullin

with a clear view out towards Whiddy Island and Bantry Bay beyond.

In 1910 John Annan Bryce and his wife Violet bought the island. They had spent summers in Glengarriff and wanted a home in West Cork. Bryce was born in Belfast, but grew up in Scotland. He was public school educated and after university went to Burma, and later India, to make his fortune. In 1888, he married Violet L'Estrange, a distant cousin of the Gore Booths of Sligo. He was elected as a Liberal Party MP for Inverness Burghs in 1906, a seat he held until 1918.

The Bryces had big plans for Ilnacullin. Both had an interest in gardening, and to help achieve their vision for the island they appointed the architect and garden designer, Harold Peto. He had designed gardens in England and the south of France. Work began in 1911 when 100 locals were employed to bring boat loads of topsoil to the island, which had virtually none. Peto then built a cottage to accommodate the Bryces until work on the planned mansion was completed. It was to incorporate the Martello tower. However the mansion was never built, as the collapse of the Russian economy where John Bryce had investments meant that he lost much of his fortune.

But before this change of plan Peto had created a walled garden, an Italianate Garden with a reflective pool and colonnade, a temple, a clock tower and a series of stepped pathways connecting each of the different gardens.

The First World War, and the death of John in 1923, meant that the gardens were neglected. Soon Violet returned to the island with her son, Roland L'Estrange Bryce, who left a distinguished career in the British Foreign Office. After the First World War he was one of the diplomats assigned to define the border for the newly created Yugoslavia. Although both were keen horticulturists, they employed Murdo MacKenzie, a Scottish botanist and horticulturalist, to come and replant and look after Ilnacullin. He remained until his death in 1983. On arrival, one of the first things he planted was rows of conifers at the edges of the island to provide shelter for the smaller shrubs. He then planted azaleas, camellias, rhododendrons and other non-native subtropical plants that thrived in the mild temperate climate of West Cork.

After Violet died in 1939, Roland continued the work his parents had started, living in the original cottage with MacKenzie and a housekeeper, local lady Mary O'Sullivan. On his death in 1953 he bequeathed Ilnacullin to the Irish State, on condition that Murdo and Mary could remain living there. The fledgling state required that such bequests come with sufficient funds for the future upkeep of the bequest. Roland's will had no such funds and, aware of the strict conditions, he left the island directly to the then Taoiseach, Éamon de Valera, who became the reluctant recipient. His successor, John A. Costello, was more enthusiastic and assigned the care of the island to the Department of Agriculture. Today it is in the care of the Office of Public Works.

MINING ON THE BEARA PENINSULA

The last stretch of Cork coastline before leaving the county is the remote Beara Peninsula. The name is attributed to Beara, a Spanish princess and wife of Owen Mor, King of Munster in the pre-Christian era. It is hard to believe that this peaceful remote region was the busiest mining district in nineteenth-century Ireland. Since the Bronze Age, copper has been mined along the coast of Allihies, where the telltale streak of green oxidised copper staining the red sandstone gave early prospectors a clue to the riches underneath.

In 1810 John Lavallin Puxley, a land owner, whose family came to Beara in Cromwellian times, began the process of getting investment to mine copper. Along with four local families, Puxley, later known as 'Copper John', opened five mines. He brought expert engineers and miners from Cornwall to plan the deep shafts, such as the one at Mountain Mine that went 320m underground, some of it well below sea level. Developments in steam technology led to the construction of engine houses, where steam engines operated pumps to drain water from the mines. The engine houses are still part of the architectural heritage of the landscape overlooking the village of Allihies today. By 1812, ore extracted by The Allihies Mining Company was being exported from Ballydonegan Bay by barge to Swansea in Wales. The returning barge was laden with coal for the steam engines. The Cornish engineers, mine captains, miners and their families were accommodated in newly built houses. As most were of the Methodist faith, a chapel was also built for them.

By the 1830s, 1,500 were employed in the five mines. The fishing village of Allihies saw a surge in population as families converged on the area to avail of the mining jobs. However, while Puxley and his investors prospered, life was not so good for the Irish miners. They were not employed by the mine owners and instead had to bid daily for the various mining jobs on offer. The most dangerous jobs paid better but were given to whoever put in the lowest bid. Miners had to rent their shovels and picks, and pay for repairs to the tools. Their wives and children worked above ground separating the ore from the rubble. They bought their food from stores owned by the mine owners. No additional housing was built to accommodate the influx of workers, so many families lived in one house. In addition, conditions in the mines were dangerous and by the 1860s the workers began to rebel, organising a series of strikes, all to no avail. By the 1870s, the days of mining on the Beara Peninsula were drawing to a close. The price of copper had fallen as deposits from Chile and America flooded the market. Irish workers left Beara, taking their mining skills to Butte in Montana. The Puxleys also left Beara.

'Copper John' died in 1856 and his second son Henry Lavallin Puxley inherited the mines. The family lived in an eighteenth-century tower house close to the ruins of the O'Sullivan Beara stronghold of Dunboy Castle, near Castletown-Berehaven. Henry transformed Puxley Manor into a lavish Neo-Gothic mansion, but when his wife died in childbirth he left Ireland. The house was abandoned and was further damaged during the War of Independence in 1921.

The Cornish writer Daphne du Maurier was friendly with the Puxleys. Her novel, *Hungry Hill*, published in 1943, although set in Cornwall, is based on their story on the Beara Peninsula.

3

COUNTY KERRY

SNEEM: THE STATUES AND MONUMENTS OF SNEEM

Sneem, with its two village squares either side of the bridge spanning the often gushing Sneem river, can boast connections with famous statesmen, not so famous sportsmen and even a spy. Some are commemorated in monuments and statues. The spy is not.

On the South Square a metal structure depicting the local mountains commemorates Cearbhall Ó'Dálaigh, who served as President of Ireland from 1974 to 1976. An eminent lawyer, he was Chief Justice of Ireland from 1961 to 1973, and then served as a Judge of the Supreme Court between 1973 and 1974. He did not serve his full term as President, as he resigned following a controversy over the Emergency Powers Bill of 1976.

At that time the Northern Ireland troubles were escalating. The Irish Government declared a state of emergency following the murder in Dublin of the recently appointed British Ambassador to Ireland, Sir Christopher Ewart Biggs. The Government drew up the Emergency Powers Bill and sent it to President Ó'Dálaigh for his signature to make it an act of law. He felt that parts of the bill were unconstitutional and, as was his right, he referred the bill to the Supreme Court. The Minister of Defence, Paddy Donegan, called the President 'a thundering disgrace' for his decision. A vote of confidence in Donegan was passed in Dáil Éireann. President Ó'Dálaigh felt his position was untenable and resigned on 22 October, the only President to have ever done so. He retired to Sneem, where he died in 1978. He is buried in the local cemetery. On the North Square The Steel Tree sculpture was presented to the town by the people of Israel in memory of Ó'Dálaigh, in recognition of his close connection with the Jewish community in Dublin. It was unveiled by Chaim Hertzog, President of Israel, who was a friend of the late President, in 1985.

Another president, who also resigned from office, is commemorated in a monument, also on the North Square of Sneem. In April 1969, after ten years in office, French President Charles De Gaulle resigned. He decided to get away from France as the election for his successor was held. He came to Ireland in search of peace and solace and found it on a six-week trip. Ireland was not a random choice as he already had a number of Irish connections, particularly with Co. Kerry. De Gaulle's interest in Ireland may have been piqued from reading a book *Le Libérateur de l'Irlande*, which his paternal grandmother, Joséphine Maillot, wrote in 1881 about Daniel O'Connell. But maybe it was his wife, Yvonne, who yearned to see Sneem, as her former nanny came from the village. In 1994, on the twenty-fifth anniversary of his visit, a memorial was erected in the village. The inscription is a quote from De Gaulle, which reads: 'At this grave moment of my long life, I found here what I sought, to be face to face with myself, Ireland gave me that, in the most delicate, the most friendly way.'

Two sports figures are commemorated in statues on the South Square. 'The Crusher' Casey, a wrestler, was born in Sneem in 1908 and in 1938 he became the World Heavyweight Wrestling Champion. The other statue is of John Egan, a Gaelic football player who won six All-Ireland Gaelic Football medals playing for Kerry in the 1970s.

One Sneem native not commemorated in a statue is William Melville, born in 1850. The son of a local baker, one day he was sent to Killarney with a cart of produce but never returned home. He had decided to go to London, where he joined the Metropolitan Police, working his way to detective sergeant with the Criminal Detective Department. He transferred into a new unit known as Special Branch, set up specifically to foil the activities of Irish Fenians in England. Melville opposed the terrorist activities of the Fenians and was able to use his Irish connections to infiltrate the movement with informers. In 1887 he helped to expose an assassination attempt on Queen Victoria, known as the Jubilee Plot. It turns out the plot was masterminded not by Irish dissidents but by the British State to undermine Charles Stewart Parnell and his Home Rule movement. With his name in the newspapers, Melville had legions of fans, who were disappointed to hear of his retirement from the police in 1903. He was not, in fact, retiring. He had been recruited by the War Office to head a new intelligence-gathering service, which would later become MI5 and MI6. Melville is thought to have been the inspiration for Ian Fleming's character M in the James Bond novels.

COOMAKISTA PASS: JADOTVILLE

The highest point along the Ring of Kerry, the Coomakista Pass affords views over Scarriff Bay to the south and Ballinskelligs Bay towards the village of Waterville. In the valley sweeping down to Ballinskelligs Bay is Loher ring fort, dating from the eighth century and recently reconstructed. On the roadside at the pass is a statue of the Blessed Virgin Mary. This is one of hundreds erected in towns and on roadsides around Ireland in 1954 when Pope Pius XII designated it a Marian Year.

The most recent feature of this perfect spot, which showcases the best of the Wild Atlantic Way scenery, is the memorial to Colonel Pat Quinlan, born in the locality in 1919 and commemorating his role in the Siege of Jadotville.

Jadotville is in the province of Katanga in the Democratic Republic of Congo (DRC) in Central Africa. In 1960 the United Nations Security Council sent soldiers from various countries, including Ireland, to assist the Congolese government in establishing a new state following recent independence from Belgium. Ireland, as a relatively new state itself, had joined the UN in 1955, and this was the first overseas mission for Irish soldiers.

However, a civil war erupted in the DRC when Moise Tshombe, a political leader in Katanga, declared independence from the DRC. Katanga, in the south-east of the country, is rich in copper and uranium. The uranium used in the atomic bombs dropped on Nagasaki and Hiroshima in 1945 came from there. With the backing of Belgian mining interests, Belgian soldiers and European mercenaries, Tshombe intended keeping the wealth generated from the valuable mines in Katanga.

In 1961, as part of the UN mission, 'A' Company of the Irish Army's 35th Infantry Battalion, under the command of Commandant Pat Quinlan, arrived in the DRC and was immediately sent to Jadotville in Katanga. The remit of the battalion, made up of soldiers from the Western Command based at Custume Barracks, Athlone, was to protect the local white community. Commandant Quinlan was immediately aware of the local community's open hostility to the UN presence. He immediately ordered his men to dig trenches and create defences at the exposed Irish compound near

Jadotville in preparation for a possible attack. Within days
'A' Company came under fire from Katanga Gendarmerie, led
by European mercenaries. The initial attack happened while
most of the Irish soldiers were attending Mass. Although
they had never experienced combat before, they rose to the
challenge. As peacekeepers, they valiantly defended themselves,
while trying to avoid unnecessary casualties on their attackers.
For six days Commandant Quinlan and his battalion of 157
men came under fire from heavy artillery. When the besieged
Irish soldiers ran out of ammunition and food, Commandant
Quinlan surrendered to the mercenaries. During the siege, five
Irish soldiers were wounded, while approximately 300 died
in the fighting on the Katangese side. The UN negotiated the
release of the Irish hostages, who were freed five weeks later.

Sadly, on returning home, there were no congratulations
or medals awarded to Commandant Quinlan or his men. His
leadership and tactics, and their bravery in fending off an army
of 3,000 at Jadotville without losing a single Irish life, went
unreported. The UN and the Irish Army preferred that the whole
affair be forgotten about. Commander Quinlan's decision to
surrender to save the lives of his men was regarded as cowardly
and had put the UN in the undignified position of having to
negotiate with the Katangese rebels. The Siege of Jadotville
was regarded as a shameful incident by the Irish Army and was
airbrushed from the army's history. Thankfully, that changed
when the book *The Siege of Jadotville* by Declan Power and the
subsequent film starring Jamie Dornan popularised the story
and highlighted the heroism of Commandant Quinlan and his
men. He is commemorated in a plaque unveiled at Coomakista
in 2017.

WATERVILLE: CHARLIE CHAPLIN

While one of the two statues along the seafront at Waterville commemorates Mick O'Dwyer, a local Gaelic footballing legend, the other attracts more attention from passing tourists. They wonder why there is a statue of Charlie Chaplin, depicted as his most iconic character, the Tramp, wearing baggy trousers, sporting a derby hat and leaning on a cane, in this quiet Kerry village.

Chaplin was married to Oona O'Neill, daughter of the playwright Eugene O'Neill, who was the son of Irish emigrants. Oona wanted to visit Ireland. Their friend Walt Disney had just returned from Ireland, where he got the inspiration to make a film about leprechauns, *Darby O'Gill and the Little People*. At his suggestion, the Chaplins and their eight children went to Kerry in the spring of 1959.

One day they were driving the Ring of Kerry and decided to stop at Waterville. Chaplin went into the Butler Arms Hotel to enquire if they had any vacancies. The receptionist told him that the hotel was fully booked, so he and his family left, heading towards Sneem. When the hotel owner, Mr Huggard, learnt that Chaplin had been turned away, he drove after them, persuaded the Chaplins to return to Waterville with him and provided them with accommodation in his family quarters. Thus began a lifelong friendship between the two families, and up until 1971 the Chaplin family came to Waterville every Easter, always staying in the Butler Arms. The children enjoyed fishing and horse riding, and while Charlie also went fishing, he was apparently not very successful at it. He and Oona also liked to take drives around the Ring of Kerry. Sadly the annual visits stopped when the Northern Ireland troubles escalated during the 1970s.

VALENTIA ISLAND: TELEGRAPH CABLE STATION AT VALENCIA ISLAND

Valentia Island gets its name from the Irish 'Inse Beal', or 'Island at the Mouth (of the bay)'. The island is 11km long, 3km wide and is linked to the mainland by a bridge to the south at Portmagee. This small corner of Ireland played an important role in the development of international telecommunications.

Throughout the nineteenth century, telegraph poles carrying wires began to sprawl across American and European countries. Messages transmitted in Morse Code were sent along the wires, between telegraph stations, where the messages were deciphered. News and information had never travelled so fast. The next challenge was to connect countries across seas. In 1851, a cable was laid in the English Channel connecting England and France with telegraph messaging. The next question was, could continents be connected in the same way?

Cyrus Field West, an American entrepreneur, who made his fortune in the paper industry, had the wealth, the connections and the vision to explore the possibility of linking North America with Europe, using a submarine telegraph cable. A survey of the Atlantic Ocean revealed that a ridge running across it, between Ireland and Canada, was the most obvious route for laying a cable. Valentia Island, in Co. Kerry, and Heart's Content, in Newfoundland, were chosen as sites for the transmitting stations. The next challenge was making and insulating a copper cable, 4,000 km long, that could withstand the pressure of tonnes of seawater. Any split or break in the cable would render it useless.

In July 1857, two ships, USS *Niagara* and HMS *Agamemnon*, left Valentia, each carrying half of the enormous cable. One ship laid cable from Valentia, and mid-Atlantic, it was to be spliced with the one on the other ship, which would then continue laying the cable to Newfoundland. However, midway across the Atlantic, the cable snapped as it was being reeled out and the venture sank with the cable into the Atlantic.

However, the future of telecommunications depended on successfully laying a transatlantic cable. The same team was ready to try again, in 1858, only this time the ships met mid-Atlantic, where the cable was successfully spliced. On 16 August 1858, the first transatlantic message was relayed. The Knight of Kerry, Peter Fitzgerald, did the honours with the following message: 'Glory to God on high, Peace on earth to men and goodwill.' This was quickly followed by a message from Queen Victoria to the President of the United States of America, James Buchanan. However, the jubilation did not last long, as soon after the cable went dead.

Over the next few years, leading scientists came together to discuss why the cable had failed. William Thomson, a Belfast-born scientist, now working in Glasgow, advised that more copper cables, twisted together, with better insulation, were required. Investors knew that a cable could be laid and were willing to put up the money for a third attempt. Laying Thomson's heavier cable required the biggest ship available, which, in 1866, was Isambard Kingdom Brunel's SS *Great Eastern*. On 27 July, with 1,600 nautical miles of cable laid behind it, the *Great Eastern* reached Heart's Content. North America and Europe once again had a telegraph connection, but one that would endure. On the first day of operation, the Atlantic Telegraph Company made £1,000. By 1870, Valentia Island was the centre of intercontinental communications. A compound of work and dwelling houses was constructed near Knightstown to accommodate staff. The station remained in operation until 1966.

Valentia's contribution to telecommunications does not end there. The next phase of telecommunications technology was wireless radio signals. In 1912, the British Post Office set up a wireless Coast Watch Service at Crookhaven, Co. Cork, where a frequency was kept open for emergencies. At the outbreak of the First World War, the service was moved to a new facility on Valentia Island, where it still operates today, taking emergency distress signals and sending help to stricken vessels, from Malin Head to Mizen Head. In May 1915, a message was sent from here to *Lusitania*, warning her that there was submarine activity in the area. The Valentia station was one of the last to use Morse Code as communications moved to using satellites, with the last message relayed on 1 February 1999.

VALENTIA ISLAND AND ITS PART IN THE 1916 EASTER RISING

When the Easter Rising of 1916 broke out, the Irish Republican Brotherhood (IRB) wanted the world to know. To that end, they enlisted the help of Tim Ring, who, with his brother Eugene, were the only Irish workers at the Transatlantic Telegraph Station on Valentia Island in 1916. Once the rebellion started, he was to message Clan na Gael members in America with the news. In preparation for this, a few days before the planned rebellion, he sent a test message to Heart's Content in Newfoundland. It read, 'Do you wish to buy a bicycle?'

The Canadian operator who received the message regarded it as irregular, so he showed it to a supervisor. As the message did not reach its intended recipient, the Rice brothers decided that dispatching the coded message about the Rising directly from Valentia would not be safe. They needed a third party to send the message to Valentia, which could then be forwarded transatlantic.

They enlisted the help of their cousin, Rosalie, who worked at the Post Office in Kenmare. When the time came, she sent the prearranged coded message, which read, 'Operation on John carried out successfully.' It was sent to John Devoy, the leader of Clan na Gael in America, and arrived on Monday, 24 April, the first day of the rebellion. Devoy was now tasked with informing the world that Ireland was in rebellion as the IRB believed that the British would not broadcast the news.

Later that year, the Ring brothers were accused of sending the message and were arrested on 15 August. Tim was sent to Frongach Prison and Eugene was held in Caherciveen barracks. Tim was released in May 1917, and as operators were scarce in wartime he was re-employed in the accounts department of the telegraph service in London.

CAHERCIVEEN: DANIEL O'CONNELL

The main thoroughfare in Dublin is named after Daniel O'Connell. Around the base of the statue dedicated to him on O'Connell Street are four statues of Nike the Greek goddess in the poses of Eloquence, Courage, Patriotism and Fidelity, the characteristics of this remarkable, early nineteenth-century, Irish politician. As an outstanding orator, he courageously took on the establishment, fighting to release Irish Catholics from the Penal Laws, which since the end of the seventeenth century had prohibited Catholics from becoming members of professions or Members of Parliament, from education and from owning land over a certain value.

He was born to a Catholic family in a humble stone cottage outside Caherciveen on 6 August 1775. His wealthy uncle, Muiris O'Connell, of Derrynane House, paid for his education at St Omer and Douai in France. By the early 1790s, France was rumbling with revolution, so O'Connell travelled to London (on the same boat carrying news to England of the execution of Louis XVI), where he trained as a lawyer, a profession that had only just begun accepting Catholics into its ranks.

He returned to Ireland to practise law. It was the passing of the Act of Union of 1800, which dissolved the Dublin Parliament, that led to O'Connell taking an active part in Irish politics. He was opposed to the Union, but knew that before it could be repealed he would have to campaign for Catholic emancipation and a lifting of the Penal Laws. Only when Catholics could vote could the Union be repealed.

In 1823 he set up the Catholic Association, collecting a penny a month from every Catholic in Ireland, to fund his campaign. His aim was to peacefully mobilise the masses to achieve his objective. In 1828, he put himself forward for election to the parliamentary seat for Co. Clare. The law did not prohibit Catholics from standing for election, it just did not allow them to take their seat in Parliament. He won, with a huge majority. The House of Commons passed the Catholic Emancipation Act of 1829, enabling him to represent his constituents. King George IV, who opposed emancipation, suggested that O'Connell and not him was 'King of Ireland'.

His next campaign was the repeal of the Act of Union and the restoration of an independent parliament in Dublin. Through mass meetings, he spread the word of the need for Repeal but the Government outlawed these gatherings and he was arrested and charged with seditious conspiracy. O'Connell represented himself at the trial, where he was found guilty and served a short prison sentence. His final years saw a split in the Repeal movement, with a younger generation advocating the use of violence, to which O'Connell was vehemently opposed. With his health failing, he went on a pilgrimage to Rome, but died in Genoa in 1847. His heart is buried in Rome and his body is buried in Glasnevin Cemetery, in Dublin, a cemetery that he had founded.

He had never forgotten his Kerry roots. In 1825, he inherited his uncle's house at Derrynane and visited it regularly throughout his life. The Daniel O'Connell Memorial Church, in Caherciveen, is the only Catholic church in Ireland named after a layperson.

MONSIGNOR HUGH O'FLAHERTY

Monsignor Hugh O'Flaherty's story begins in Killarney, where he was born in 1898. His father worked at the local golf club, instilling a love of the game in the Monsignor, who would, in later life, become an amateur golf champion. During his time in Rome, he played golf with ex-King Alfonso of Spain and Count Ciano, son-in-law of Mussolini. But this is not why his life is remarkable.

Monsignor O'Flaherty first went to Rome in 1922. On his ordination, in 1925, he was assigned to the Vatican's Diplomatic Service. After serving in Haiti, Santa Domingo and Czechoslovakia, he returned to the Vatican, just before the outbreak of the Second World War. It was during the war that he made the most significant contribution of his life. As the Nazis descended on Rome, the Vatican City remained a neutral state. Soon, the Monsignor was helping refugees, prisoners of war and Jewish people to flee the tyranny of the Nazis. He was helped by the British Ambassador, Sir Francis D'Arcy Osborne, who was taking refuge in the Vatican, and the wife of the Irish Ambassador to the Vatican, the singer Delia Murphy. Together, they set up the Rome Escape Line, which smuggled refugees into the neutral territory of the Vatican. A white line on the ground outside the Vatican marked where that neutral territory began and the Nazi-controlled Rome ended.

This activity soon brought Monsignor O'Flaherty to the attention of Colonel Herbert Kappler, the head of the SS in Rome, who saw the Irish priest as a thorn in his side. To coordinate rescue efforts, Monsignor O'Flaherty had to venture into occupied Rome and during these visits he took to disguising himself. On one occasion he entered Rome dressed as a nun and on another he hid in a coal chute to escape capture. Small wonder then that he became known as the Scarlet Pimpernel of the Vatican.

Over 4,000 people were saved from certain death at the hands of the Nazis thanks to the efforts of Monsignor O'Flaherty but his humanitarianism did not end there. As the Allies descended on Rome, he helped Colonel Kappler to get his family safely home to Germany. Kappler himself was later captured, tried and sentenced to life in prison, where Monsignor O'Flaherty visited him once a month. Kappler later converted to Catholicism.

After suffering a stroke, Monsignor O'Flaherty returned to Ireland and to Caherciveen, to live with his sister. He died there in October 1963 and is buried in the grounds of the Daniel O'Connell Memorial Church. In the 1980s, Gregory Peck played the role of Monsignor O'Flaherty in the film *The Scarlet and the Black*.

KILLORGLIN: THE FIRST CASUALTIES
OF THE 1916 EASTER RISING

Shortly before the 1916 Easter Rising, a Kerry-based member of the Irish Volunteers, Con Keating, was sent to Dublin to get instructions for a special mission being assigned to him by the IRB. On Good Friday he travelled to Limerick by train, accompanied by Donal Sheehan from Newcastle West in Co. Limerick and Charlie Monahan from Belfast. Each of them had a skill that was crucial to their mission. Keating had worked on ships as a radio operator, Sheehan's work at the British War Office meant he had knowledge of British Admiralty codes, and Monahan was a skilled wireless technician. They were on their way to Caherciveen to steal wireless equipment from the wireless training school where Keating had been trained.

The trio were met at Limerick Station by two cars. Tom McInerney was to drive the car carrying the wireless team, while Dennis Daly and Colm O'Lochlainn, who knew the Kerry roads, would lead the way. As they were travelling in the dark, McInerney was instructed to keep the taillights of the lead vehicle in view. Needless to say, they lost each other along the winding roads of Kerry. The first car had passed through Killorglin before realising that the second car was not behind. They pulled over, waiting for McInerney to catch up. Not wanting to attract attention and with no sign of the second car, Daly and O'Lochlainn continued along the road, assuming that the mission had been aborted.

The second car had got lost. On the Milltown side of Killorglin, McInerney pulled over to ask a young girl for directions to Caherciveen. She told them to cross the bridge in Killorglin and then turn right, after the bridge. This they did, but instead of following the curve of the road, McInerney drove straight on, towards Ballykissane Pier. In the dark McInerney thought the moon was reflecting off the wet road ahead, when in fact it was shining on the River Laune. The car careered off the pier and plunged into the freezing water. The only survivor was McInerney. He managed to get ashore and was taken to the local Royal Irish Constabulary station. There, he told the officers that he did not know the deceased, as they were tourists visiting Kerry for the Easter weekend, and he had been hired to drive them. The following day, two of the bodies were recovered from the Laune by fishermen (the third body was not found until October) and documents found on them identified them as Irish Volunteers. McInerney was arrested and following the Rising he was sent, like other Irish Volunteers, to Frongach Prison, in North Wales.

Why were they stealing wireless equipment? The plan was to transmit messages to the Royal Navy, alerting them, falsely, of a plan by the German Navy to attack Scottish naval bases. It was believed that such news would distract the Admiralty away from the Irish coast and allow a shipment of weapons from Germany to be landed at Banna Strand.

ANNASCAUL: TOM CREAN

Tom Crean was born near Annascaul in 1877. He is the unsung hero of Antarctic exploration, having spent more time in Antarctica than either Robert Falcon Scott or Ernest Shackleton, the more famous explorers with whom he travelled.

Crean left the Dingle Peninsula at the age of 15 and, lying about his age, joined the Royal Navy. His Antarctic adventures began in 1901. He was a petty officer 2nd class on board the Royal Navy ship *Ringaroome*, which was docked at Lyttelton in New Zealand when Scott docked with *Discovery*. He was en route to Antarctica, the last great undiscovered region of the world. While in Lyttelton, one of his crew punched an officer and absconded, leaving Scott short a crew member. He persuaded the captain of *Ringaroome* to transfer Crean to *Discovery*, and thus began the Kerryman's Antarctic adventures.

This first trip to Antarctica resulted in the ship being trapped in ice for almost two years. While Crean accompanied treks made across the icy wastes in the hope of reaching the South Pole, Scott and his team were not successful on this occasion. They returned to Portsmouth in 1904 and Tom Crean was promoted to petty officer 1st class.

He travelled with Scott again, in 1910, on *Terra Nova*. This time Scott was determined to be the first man to reach the South Pole. Crean got to within 240 km of the ultimate goal, but was not chosen for the six-man team that would make the final push. On Crean's way back to base camp he had an adventure of his own. Accompanying him was Lieutenant Evans, who collapsed on the way. Crean trekked 56 km through an icy wasteland in hazardous weather conditions to get help. The trek took him eighteen hours.

He was later awarded the Albert Medal for Lifesaving.

In the meantime, on 17 January 1912, Scott and his team reached the South Pole. But there they found the Norwegian flag that Roald Amundsen and his team had pitched five weeks earlier. A despondent Scott and his team began the arduous trek back to their base camp. Just

18 km short of safety, they ran into a snowstorm and all perished. Tom Crean was in the team that found and buried the body of 'Scott of the Antarctic'.

Crean was not done with Antarctica and his biggest adventure was yet to come. In 1914, he sailed with Ernest Shackleton to the Southern Hemisphere on board *Endurance*. The ship became icebound in the Waddell Sea, leaving the crew marooned on Elephant Island. In a tiny lifeboat, *James Caird*, with Shackleton and Worsley, Crean crossed 1290 km of the South Atlantic, one of the most dangerous stretches of water in the world, to get help for twenty-two stranded colleagues. Unfortunately, when they reached South Georgia they landed on the uninhabited side of the island and faced a 64-km walk, across glaciers and mountains. However, their bid was successful and all were saved.

Crean spent twenty-seven years in the Royal Navy, reaching the rank of warrant officer. He retired in 1920 and returned to his native Kerry, where he opened the South Pole Inn at Annascaul. Once home, Crean did not talk much about his Antarctic adventures. The political situation in Ireland at that time meant that his service with the Royal Navy would have been a contentious subject in the early years of Irish independence. It is indeed tragic that, after all the near-death experiences he encountered in his twenty-year naval career he should die at home of a ruptured appendix in 1938.

WHY QUEEN MARIE ANTOINETTE NEVER CAME TO DINGLE

During her captivity following the French Revolution, there were a number of plots to rescue Queen Marie Antoinette from Paris. One such plot, had it been successful, would have brought her to Dingle in Co. Kerry.

The mastermind behind this 1792 plot was James Louis Rice. He was born into a Catholic merchant family in Dingle in 1730. His father, known locally as Black Tom, imported wine from Spain and France. With his contacts on the Continent, Black Tom sent James to Louvain in Belgium to train for the priesthood. Rice, however, had other plans, and instead joined the Austrian Army. As an exemplary soldier, he quickly rose through the ranks. Also serving in his regiment was Joseph II, Emperor of Austria, with whom he became friendly. Soon James Rice, from Dingle, was moving in royal circles.

Joseph II was Marie Antoinette's brother and he was anxious to rescue her when the French Revolution broke out. In June 1791, King Louis XVI and Marie Antoinette had attempted to flee Paris but were stopped and arrested at the village of Varennes. They were brought back to Paris and confined to the Tuileries Palace until mobs stormed the palace in August 1792. While the Royal family were incarcerated at the Temple prison, a French Republic was declared. The King and Queen were tried and found guilty of treason. Their lives were now in great danger.

Rice meticulously planned a rescue mission for his friend's sister. He planned to disguise himself as a Frenchman and bribe the prison guards to turn a blind eye while the Queen was spirited away. He had secured a coach and arranged replacement horses along the route from Paris to Nantes. At Nantes, one of his father's ships was waiting to take the Queen to the safety of Dingle, where James Rice had rooms prepared for her at his house in the town. From Dingle, the Queen would travel to Vienna, via London and Brussels. The plan would have been a success, but Rice, and those helping him, had not accounted for one detail. Queen Marie Antoinette refused to leave Paris without her husband and children. As they were all imprisoned separately, and the original plan was for the rescue of just one person, the whole escapade was abandoned. Louis XVI was executed by guillotine in January 1793 and Marie Antoinette, who could have avoided the same fate, was executed in October 1793.

BANNA STRAND: EVENTS IN COUNTY KERRY DURING THE 1916 EASTER RISING

At the outbreak of the First World War thousands of Irish men joined the fray and fought in the trenches alongside soldiers from all parts of the British Isles. Meanwhile, others in Ireland saw the distraction of war as the ideal time to rise up against British rule and fight for an independent Ireland. The leadership of the Irish Republican Brotherhood (IRB) decided that Easter 1916 was the ideal time to call to arms the Irish Volunteers and the Irish Citizen Army. The job of securing sufficient weapons for the success of the rebellion was given to Sir Roger Casement.

Casement was a former official with the British Foreign Service, who was knighted in 1911 for his work in highlighting atrocities carried out in the Belgian Congo by the authorities against native workers. An Irish Nationalist and a member of the Irish Volunteers, he undertook the treasonable journey to Germany in the hope of persuading the authorities there to provide weapons for the Rising. On 30 March 1916, a former British-registered steamer, SS *Castro*, which the Germans had captured in their territorial waters at the start of the war, was loaded with 20,000 rifles, a dozen machine guns, and 1 million rounds of ammunition, and set sail for Ireland. Sailing under a Norwegian flag, and renamed *Aud*, she was also carrying a cargo of household goods to conceal the cache of weapons.

With Captain Spindler at the helm, *Aud* sailed into the North Sea, navigating her way down the west coast of Ireland. Meanwhile, Casement was returning to Ireland on board the German submarine *U19*. The two vessels were to rendezvous at a point off Inistooskert, one of the Blasket Islands, on Good Friday. Irish Volunteers, on the coast near Fenit, were to signal the vessels that it was safe to come ashore.

As Captain Spindler passed the Co. Clare coast, he decided to throw some of the camouflage cargo overboard to make it easier to offload the weapons later. However, guards at the Signal Station at Loop Head alerted the Admiralty to the ship's presence in Irish waters and her odd activity. Skipper John Donaldson, from the patrol vessel *Setter II*, boarded *Aud* for an inspection but he did not find anything amiss with the 'Norwegian' cargo ship and sent her on her way.

On the night of Thursday, 20 April 1916, Spindler came close to Fenit harbour and waited for the submarine and the signal from the shore. As Good Friday dawned, with no sign of the submarine and no signal from the shore, he sailed back out to sea. The submarine was not far away but they missed each other. The shore signal did not happen because those tasked with the job had got the date wrong.

At sea, Spindler was ordered to stop by the British naval patrol vessel *Lord Heneage*. Captain Spindler ignored the order and was soon being pursued by every British naval vessel in the vicinity. Eventually, HMS *Bluebell* and HMS *Zinnea* caught up with him and escorted him to Cork Harbour. On Saturday, 22 April, just before they reached the harbour, Spindler and his crew abandoned ship into lifeboats, but not before they had discarded the Norwegian flag and replaced it with a German naval ensign. *Aud* exploded and sank, her cargo of weapons, intended for the Easter Rising, sinking to the seabed along with her.

In the meantime, *U19*'s commander, Raimund Weisbach, who had been the torpedo officer on *U20*, which had sunk *Lusitania* less than a year earlier, did not want to wait around. Casement was put in a dinghy and came ashore at Banna Strand. Constable Bernard Reilly, of Ardfert Royal Irish Constabulary Station, was alerted to the dinghy and met Casement walking along a road. He initially pretended to be someone else and claimed to be in the district researching a book on St Brendan. However, he was arrested and his identity verified. Sir Roger Casement had consorted with the enemy and was tried for treason under the Treason Act of 1351. He was hanged at Pentonville Prison on 3 August 1916. The 1916 Easter Rising went ahead on Easter Monday, despite not having the weapons from Germany.

In 2012, *Aud*'s anchors were taken from their watery grave in Cork Harbour. One is in Cobh and the other is in Blennerville, Co. Kerry.

BALLYLONGFORD: THE BIRTHPLACE OF TWO VERY DIFFERENT SOLDIERS

The quiet village of Ballylongford was the birthplace of two historical figures, both of whom died in 1916. However, there the similarity ends, as Horatio Kitchener and Michael O'Rahilly would fight two very different wars during their lifetimes.

Kitchener's family came to Ballylongford when his father sold his commission in the British Army and bought property there under a scheme that offered former soldiers land in Ireland. He was born in 1850, but the family did not stay long in Kerry as the damp Atlantic air did not agree with his mother. He followed his father into the Army, rising through the ranks and making a name for himself. He was Commander-in-Chief of the British Army in Sudan in the late 1890s, defeated the Boers in South Africa in 1902 and later served in India. By 1914 at the outbreak of the First World War, he was Lord Kitchener of Khartoum and was the obvious choice for Secretary for War in Asquith's War Cabinet. He was not popular with the politicians of Westminster, especially as he predicted that the war would drag on for years, while they envisaged it being over by Christmas. On his appointment, he immediately began a recruitment campaign to build up the ranks of the British Army, using his own image on the now iconic 'Your country needs you' posters. The successful recruitment campaign made a celebrity of Kitchener, making him even more unpopular with his Cabinet colleagues.

By June 1916, his reputation was in decline, having been blamed for the Army's shortage in ammunition. He was, therefore, relieved to be sent out of London on an important mission to Archangel in Russia to meet and discuss war tactics with Britain's Russian allies. He joined HMS *Hampshire* at Scapa Flow in the Orkney Islands. The ship left in a storm and was sailing up the western side of the islands when she struck a German mine. The ship sank in fifteen minutes with the loss of over 600 lives, including that of Lord Kitchener. He was born on the Atlantic coast and died in the icy depths of the same ocean. His body was never recovered, and although many conspiracy theories abounded about his fate, there was no evidence to suggest that anything other than an act of war had sunk the *Hampshire*.

Michael Joseph Rahilly was born in Ballylongford in 1875. With a number of businesses in the area, his family were sufficiently wealthy for him to be educated at Clongowes Woods and later University College Dublin, where he trained as a doctor. O'Rahilly never worked in the profession as he had a private income of £900 from his family. He travelled to America, where he met and married a wealthy American, Nancy Browne. In 1909, he returned to Ballylongford with his wife and three sons. Nancy was not fond of living in such a remote place and the family moved to Dublin, eventually settling in Herbert Place.

There is no suggestion that O'Rahilly had any nationalist leanings before his return to Ireland. However, once home, he embraced the nationalist movement, joining the Gaelic League, Sinn Féin and the Irish Volunteers. It was around this time that he began calling himself 'The O'Rahilly', the addition of the definite article a nod to titles used by Gaelic chieftains of old.

As a member of the Irish Volunteers, he knew that a rising was being planned. However, when the shipment of weapons from Germany was intercepted, on Good Friday of 1916, Eoin McNeill, leader of the Irish Volunteers, ordered that the Rising should be called off. 'The O'Rahilly' was given the job of delivering that order to Irish Volunteers in Cork, Kerry and Tipperary. On Easter Sunday, his job done, he returned to Dublin, little knowing that the Irish Republican Brotherhood leadership had countermanded the order. He first learnt of the Rising when he heard rifle shots on that Easter Monday morning. He got in his car and drove to Liberty Hall, where he met Padraig Pearse and the other leaders. While 'The O'Rahilly' did not agree with the rebellion, he nonetheless rowed in behind the leaders, spending the week of the Rising at the General Post Office (GPO). By 29 April, the tide had turned against the rebels. 'The O'Rahilly' was sent, with a group of Volunteers, to scout an escape route out of the GPO. As they made their way down Moore Street, they were attacked by a troop of soldiers with a machine gun. 'The O'Rahilly' was wounded and slumped into a doorway, bleeding heavily. He died, lying in the street, known today as O'Rahilly Parade, a number of hours later. While dying, he managed to write a note on the envelope of a letter he had received from his son. The note was delivered to his wife Nancy, and in it he explained that he had been shot and said of the Rising, 'It was a good fight.' Although Nancy wanted him to be buried in Ballylongford, the IRB leadership persuaded her to have him laid to rest in Glasnevin Cemetery, Dublin.

4

COUNTY LIMERICK AND COUNTY CLARE

THE FLYING BOATS AT FOYNES

When Alcock and Brown flew their Vickers Vimy biplane non-stop across the Atlantic in 1919, the race was on to build aircraft that could carry passengers between America and Europe. By landing on a bog in Clifden, Ireland's part in the future of aviation was assured. During the 1930s, the hydrogen-filled airship looked like being the future of intercontinental passenger air travel, that is until the *Hindenburg* disaster of 1937. The next most feasible option was the flying boat. These aircraft did not require the construction of a costly tarmacadam runway, all they needed to get airborne was a long, straight, calm stretch of water. They could also fly over wide bodies of water, upon which they could land should they encounter difficulties.

The Montreal Agreement of 1935 recognised Ireland as the most western landmass in Europe and chose Foynes, on the Shannon estuary, as the ideal location for a transatlantic flying boat port. Foynes had a harbour and existing road and rail connections to Limerick, and beyond. More importantly, for pilots, the water was calm and the estuary was visible from the air. The first commercial transatlantic flight left Foynes on 9 July 1937 when a Boeing 314 'Yankee Clipper' operated by Pan Am took fifteen hours to fly to America. Soon other airlines such as Imperial Airways (later British Overseas Airways Corporation [BOAC]) and Air France were operating flights between the two continents, making stops in Newfoundland during the summer and the Azores during the winter. Planes could typically accommodate thirty-six passengers, each paying a fare equivalent to €5,000 in today's money.

Hollywood stars such as Bob Hope and Douglas Fairbanks and the writer Ernest Hemingway passed through Foynes, while future US president John F. Kennedy landed there as he returned to America from Europe in 1939 at the outbreak of the Second World War. In fact, the Foynes flying boat port was at its busiest during the war years, when many Allied military and diplomatic personnel passed through the facility, the neutral Irish Government turning a blind eye.

As the Fastnet Rock off Mizen Head posed a threat to mariners, Mount Brandon on the Dingle Peninsula posed a threat to the aviators using Foynes, in the days when pilots had to visually identify hazards. In the summer of 1943, two planes crashed into the side of the Kerry mountain. On 28 July, a BOAC Sunderland flying boat, G-AGES, was travelling from Lisbon to Foynes. The flight reached the Irish coast earlier than expected and, as it was still dark, and in the absence of modern navigational aids, the pilots decided to go back out to sea and circle until daybreak before attempting a landing. Unfortunately, in the darkness the aeroplane crashed on the lower slopes of Mount Brandon. Of the eighteen passengers and seven crew on board, fifteen were killed.

Locals from the village of Cloghane climbed to the wreckage site to assist the survivors and noticed that the crash site was strewn with letters. The flight was carrying mailbags holding 30,000 letters sent from British prisoners of war held in

Japanese camps to their families in Great Britain. Realising the significance of these letters, the Kerry villagers gathered as many as they could and forwarded them to the families waiting to hear from their incarcerated loved ones. About 2,000 were collected from the mountainside. Four of those who died in the crash are buried at Killiney Churchyard near Cloghane. The headstone commemorating the four victims was paid for by BOAC. As two of the deceased were military men they are commemorated with Commonwealth War Grave Commission headstones.

While news of the July tragedy was reported internationally, the second crash, on the slopes of Mount Brandon at Slieveglass on 22 August 1943, was kept from the press. A Royal Air Force Short Sunderland, DD848, carrying a crew of eleven from 201 Squadron, crashed into the mountainside. The crew, based at Pembroke Dock in Wales, had flown out of Castle Archdale in Co. Fermanagh and were patrolling the Irish coast. Eight crew members were killed. As the plane was on military service and had crashed in a neutral country, news of the disaster was not circulated. Some of the crash victims were buried in Irvinestown in Co. Tyrone. All four of the plane's engines are still on the slopes of Mount Brandon.

The last flying boat left Foynes in 1946. Technological advances in aviation during the war meant the future of air travel was in land-based airports. A site on the west coast

of Ireland was vital for intercontinental flights and experts, such as Charles Lindbergh, chose Rinneanna, further up the Shannon estuary, as the site for a new airport.

One lasting legacy of the heyday of Foynes is the Irish coffee. That combination of Irish whiskey, coffee, sugar and a dollop of fresh Irish cream was the invention of chef Joe Sheridan, who devised it in 1942 to warm passengers at Foynes who were not used the damp chill of the Shannon air.

THE SHANNON ESTUARY: AN COLLEEN BAWN

In September 1819, the local magistrate, the Knight of Glin, was called to Moneypoint on the north shore of the Shannon Estuary. The body of a girl had been washed up and foul play was suspected. The story that unfolded would later become the subject of a novel, a play and an opera, and Ellen Hanley, the 15-year-old victim, would forever be known as the 'Colleen Bawn'.

Ellen came from Ballycahane in Co. Limerick, where she lived with her uncle. Regarded as a local beauty, she came to the attention of John Scanlan, the son of a local squire, who found her even more attractive when he learnt that her uncle had put aside a dowry for her. He proposed to her, but she was initially hesitant, possibly wondering why a member of the gentry would be interested in an uneducated country girl like her. He persisted in his suit and the couple eloped in July 1819, accompanied by Scanlan's faithful manservant Sullivan. A marriage ceremony took place in Limerick, although it was possibly not an official wedding. By the time they arrived in Glin, on the shores of the Shannon, Ellen believed that she was Mrs Scanlan. There, they stayed at a hunting lodge where Scanlan employed a local woman, Ellen Walsh, as a part-time servant.

One day they took a day trip to Kilrush on a passenger ferry. Seated next to Ellen was a Protestant clergyman in whom Ellen confided that she was not happy with her marriage, was worried that her new husband was gambling her dowry money away and regretted ever leaving her uncle's farm. She was not the only one regretting the marriage. By now, Scanlan had grown tired of his young, socially inferior bride and was plotting to get rid of her. He persuaded Sullivan to kill her, who after one failed attempt took Ellen on a boat trip, during which he bludgeoned her to death, bound her body with rope and threw her into the Shannon. Scanlan and Sullivan then fled Glin and went their separate ways.

Ellen Walsh, the Glin servant, assumed that Ellen had departed with her husband. In September 1819, she noticed a woman, Sullivan's sister, wearing a cloak that she knew belonged to Ellen. Concerned that perhaps something sinister had happened to Ellen, she informed the local magistrate, the Knight of Glin. Not long afterwards he was called to Moneypoint to view the female corpse that had washed up on the shore. He asked his friend, a Protestant clergyman, to accompany him, telling him that he expected it to be Ellen. This prompted his friend to recount his meeting with a sad girl on a boat earlier in the year.

Ellen Walsh's description of Ellen Hanley's protruding teeth led to her identification. When a local boatman, who had a particular way of splicing rope, identified the rope bound around Ellen's body as one he had given to Scanlan in July 1819, a warrant was issued for the arrests of Scanlan and Sullivan. Scanlan was later found hiding out at the family home in Co. Limerick, whereupon he was arrested and tried for murder. His defence barrister was Daniel O'Connell and it was assumed that as he was a member of the landed gentry he would be acquitted. However, the evidence against him was damning and Scanlan was found guilty and hanged for Ellen's murder. Sullivan was later found in Tralee Jail, where, using a false name, he was in prison for using fake banknotes. He too was charged with Ellen's murder. As he went to the gallows he confessed to killing Ellen, but said he had done it for Scanlan.

The term 'Colleen Bawn' was first used in a novel based on the tragedy published almost a decade later. In his book *The Collegians*, Limerick writer Gerard Griffin moved the location of the story from the banks of the Shannon to the Lakes of Killarney. Thirty years later the playwright Dion Boucicault wrote a play called *The Colleen Bawn*, which was performed in New York and London and was seen three times by Queen Victoria. In 1862, Julius Benedict composed the opera *The Lily of Killarney*, again based on Griffin's novel.

Ellen was buried in Killimer cemetery, Co. Clare, in a grave provided by Peter O'Connell, a local schoolmaster who, like so many others in Ireland, was appalled at the savage murder of a young girl. Today, a bust of the 'Colleen Bawn' in the cemetery looks out over the waters where she died.

SCATTERY ISLAND

A mile off the coast of Kilrush, at the mouth of the Shannon estuary, lies Scattery Island, a small island with a big history. The built heritage includes the ruins of an early Christian monastic site, an eighteenth-century defence battery, a nineteenth-century lighthouse and an abandoned village.

The sixth-century monastery was founded by St Senan, who was guided to the highest point of the island by an angel and there he killed An Cathach, a sea monster that was terrorising the coast. A strict disciplinarian, one of St Senan's rules decreed that no woman should be allowed on the island. When he died in AD 544 he was buried on Scattery. In the following centuries the cult of St Senan led to an expansion of the monastery, with the addition of more churches. Some miracles have been attributed to the good saint, most notably in 1864 when a local woman was cured of paralysis after she spent a night sleeping on St Senan's grave.

The tallest building on the island, which can be seen from the mainland, is the well-preserved round tower, dating from around AD 800 and thought to be one of the earliest in Ireland. The round towers were the bell towers of the early Christian monasteries. While the doorway of most Irish round towers is located about 4m above the ground, unusually, the door of the Scattery Island tower is at ground level. At the top of the tower there are four windows, one each looking north, south, east and west.

Did a monk, looking from these windows in AD 816 know the trouble that lay ahead when he saw a Viking longboat enter the estuary? More than a century of Viking raids followed, until AD 954, when they settled on the island to watch over the boats plying their way up and down the Shannon, to and from the Viking trading town of Limerick, some 60km upstream.

The Vikings on Scattery, in turn, came under attack in AD 978, from the King of Munster, Brian Boru, who killed Imar of Limerick and hundreds of his followers. He would later, as High King of Ireland, defeat the Vikings again, in 1014, at the Battle of Clontarf in Dublin. More upheaval came to Scattery with the arrival of William Hoel, an Anglo-Norman, who destroyed many of the monastic buildings. By the sixteenth century the monastery was reduced to a collection of ruined churches, six of which can still be seen on the island today.

At the end of the eighteenth century, and with a threat of French invasion, the British built a semicircular battery and accommodation for twenty soldiers. It was one of many batteries and watchtowers built along the west coast in the Napoleonic era. When the threat receded after the Battle of Waterloo in 1815, the island was abandoned.

However, a small community returned to the island in 1842. An 1823 Act of Parliament required all ships using the Shannon estuary to take a local pilot on board. Most pilots lived in Kilbaha, a village further up the coast. On seeing a ship, the pilots were rowed out to sea in currachs, racing each other, as the first pilot to reach the ship was given the piloting job. In 1842, a cargo ship, *The Windsor Castle*, was en route to Liverpool from Bombay, laden with cotton, sugar and spices, when she was struck by another boat in the English Channel. Her crew abandoned ship and the seas carried *The Windsor Castle* to Co. Clare. The pilots of Kilbaha boarded her and brought her to safety off Scattery Island, claiming salvage rights. After a legal battle, thirty-four men were awarded over £100 each. They used the money to buy land on Scattery Island, where they built homes. Their working lives were safer, as they could now row to the approaching ships in the calmer waters of the Shannon estuary. In 1866 plans for a lighthouse on the island were drawn up and it was ready for service in 1872. By 1881, 141 people lived on Scattery Island, made up of pilots, lighthouse keepers and their families, but in the twentieth century the population would decline. In 1954 the Limerick Harbour Master decided that pilots needed a motorised launch to reach the ships as the traditional currach was no longer suitable. With no accessible pier on the island, the service moved to Kilrush and the last two inhabitants left the island in 1978.

Today, Scattery Island is in the care of the Irish State where, during the summer months, a ferry operates from Kilrush bringing visitors to this island to see its 1,200 years of built heritage.

KILRUSH: THE FLIGHTY BOY

John Francis O'Reilly was born in Kilrush in 1916. His father, as a Royal Irish Constabulary officer, was one of the officers who arrested Sir Roger Casement that year. During the 1930s O'Reilly tried numerous careers before gaining notoriety as an unsuccessful German spy during the Second World War. It is little wonder that he came to be known as 'The Flighty Boy'.

After leaving school he started working in the Civil Service. Not happy there, he went to England, where he joined a monastery but after three weeks decided monastic life was not for him. He then worked in hotels in the south-west of England, before making his way to the Channel Islands. When Jersey was occupied by the Nazis in 1940, he refused to evacuate as he did not want to return to England where he could be conscripted. Befriending a Nazi soldier who wanted to improve his English, O'Reilly hinted that he and other Irish emigrant workers, stranded on Jersey, would like to go to Germany. He was soon working at a steelworks in Brunswick (Braunschweig). He initially intended earning enough money to return to Ireland via Portugal, but his plan changed in 1941 after a trip to Berlin, where O'Reilly was interviewed by the Ministry for Propaganda. He persuaded the Nazis that he would be an ideal spy and began his career by broadcasting Nazi propaganda over the radio. In fact, his family bought their first radio to listen to his broadcasts.

In December 1943, plans were under way to send him on a spying mission to Ireland. Equipped with a transmitter, he was to inform Berlin about Allied shipping and military movements around Ireland. He was also to infiltrate any British organisations not content with the war effort. Originally he was to travel to Ireland by submarine, but in the end he came by air and on 16 December 1943 he parachuted into his home county of Clare.

On that day, a volunteer manning the Loop Head Look-Out Post saw an unidentified aeroplane pass overhead. The same aeroplane was heard at the Garda station in Kilkee, where later that day Sergeant Dawson received reports of a stranger wearing a long grey coat and carrying a heavy suitcase walking along a country road outside the town. Sgt Dawson found O'Reilly, who when questioned openly admitted to having parachuted into Co. Clare from a German aeroplane. He was arrested under the Offences Against the State Act for illegally entering Ireland. He brazenly asked if he had landed at the designated air or sea ports, would he still have been charged? O'Reilly was brought to Arbour Hill Prison in Dublin, from where he later escaped in July 1944.

A reward of £500 was offered for his capture and posters with his picture were placed in newspapers. Eluding the authorities, he managed to travel by train to Limerick, hiding under a seat for the entire journey. A passenger noticed him and later identified him as O'Reilly. From Limerick he walked to his family home in Kilkee, where he was found by the police. His father later applied for and was granted the £500 reward money.

On his release from prison after the war, O'Reilly bought a hotel in Dublin. He died in a car accident in London in 1971 and is buried in an unmarked grave in Glasnevin Cemetery. Today the German transmitter radio that was parachuted into Ireland along with him, and which was never used, can be seen in Collins Barracks Museum, Dublin.

LOOP HEAD PENINSULA:
KILBAHA THE LITTLE ARK

By 1850, Ireland was recovering from the bleak years of
the Potato Famine. For the parishioners of Moyarta and
Kilballyowen, on the Loop Head Peninsula, however, little had
changed and they still faced hunger, disease and the threat of
eviction. In 1849, a cholera outbreak added to the distress.
As the parish priest, Fr Malachy Duggan, lay dying from the
disease, he was anointed by Fr Michael Meehan, who had
grown up in the parish and was then a curate in Kilrush. Within
days Fr Meehan succeeded his friend as parish priest of this
poor, sprawling coastal parish.

The parish had three churches, at Carrigaholt, Cross and
Doonaha, and no schools, apart from some informal 'hedge
schools'. Within a year, Fr Meehan had three National Board-
run schools operating in his parish. These schools were some
of the first in Ireland to teach the Irish language.

One of the biggest challenges he faced was the arrival of
'Souperism' in his parish. The Irish Church Mission Society
offered food, usually soup, clothing and education in the most
deprived parts of Ireland. This proselytising organisation
would only continue to feed people if they abandoned their
Catholic faith in favour of Protestantism. For Catholics
living in dire poverty it was sometimes an easy choice, and
those who chose to avail of this charity were often accused
of 'taking the soup'. To add to Fr Meehan's problems, a local
land agent on Loop Head, Marcus Keane, actively encouraged
the missionaries to set up their own schools. His tenants were
advised to send their children to these schools, rather than
the new ones Fr Meehan had founded. They were promised
that there would be no religious instruction; but soon children

were coming home with stories about being made to spit on an image of the Blessed Virgin Mary.

A battle for the souls of the Catholics of Moyarta and Kilballyowen had broken out. As part of his plan for the parish, Fr Meehan wanted to build another church near the village of Kilbaha as the nearest one to the villagers was 8 km away. However, Keane refused to grant permission for a new church and threatened to evict any tenant who held Mass in their home. When Fr Meehan took possession of two cottages abandoned by emigrating tenants and converted them into a temporary church, Keane had them flattened. However, Fr Meehan was a resourceful man and his next solution made national news.

One day he was walking along the beach in the nearby Victorian seaside resort of Kilkee when he noticed bathing boxes, a Victorian hut on wheels, which allowed a woman to enter the sea while preserving her modesty. Fr Meehan had a similar structure built by a local carpenter. His 'chapel on wheels' housed a small altar, above which he hung a crucifix. One Sunday morning, in 1852, he pitched his new 'chapel', at the crossroads in Kilbaha. A crowd gathered and through the windows on either side of the hut they could see the Mass service conducted by Fr Meehan. They were soon referring to his chapel as 'the Ark'.

Fr Meehan knew that landlords had no ownership of the public road and by pitching his chapel where the road led to the beach he was not breaking any law. Nonetheless, Keane found a reason to bring Fr Meehan before the local Petty Sessions Court, accusing him of causing an obstruction on a public road. The case was thrown out.

For five years the Catholics of Kilbaha attended Mass, weddings and christenings at Fr Meehan's Ark. News of 'the

Ark' and Fr Meehan's struggle to obtain a site soon went beyond Co. Clare and donations flooded in for a new church. One donation of £3 3s was made by members of the police service based in the Phoenix Park, Dublin. However, without a site to build on, there could be no new church.

The intervention of Keane's absentee landlord, Lord Francis Conyngham, brought a resolution to the conflict. He was contesting an election and realised that the heavy-handedness of Keane, his land agent, could affect his chances. Keane was ordered to give the priest a site. However, in one more fit of rancour, Keane offered Fr Meehan a site on bogland, which was rejected. Eventually the foundation stone for the new church was laid on 12 July 1857, at Moneen. 'The Ark' continued to be used for services until the new church, named 'Star of the Sea', was consecrated on 10 October 1858. Today, 'the Ark' can be seen in a side room of the church. A plaque on the quayside in Kilbaha acknowledges the lengths to which Fr Meehan went to protect his parishioners. He died at his sister's home in Limerick on 24 January 1878.

KILRUSH, KILKEE, MILTOWN MALBAY: PERCY FRENCH AND THE WEST CLARE RAILWAY

On 10 August 1896, the popular song writer Percy French set out from Dublin by train. He was on his way to perform at Moore's Hall in Kilkee at 8 p.m. that evening. A native of Co. Roscommon, French had trained as a civil engineer and got a job as inspector of drains in Co. Cavan on graduation, but left it to become editor of a Dublin-based comic magazine called *The Jarvey*. In Dublin he began organising concerts, where he performed humorous self-penned songs. When the magazine closed, he began performing full time and by 1896 was filling music halls the length and breadth of Ireland. The audience at Kilkee was no doubt looking forward to hearing him perform popular songs, such as *The Mountains of Mourne* and *Slattery's Mounted Fut.*

According to the train timetable, he would arrive in Kilkee at 3.30 p.m., which gave him plenty of time to prepare for his performance. The Dublin train arrived in Ennis and Percy French comfortably connected with the West Clare Railway to continue to Kilkee. At 3 p.m., at the village of Miltown Malbay, 30 km from Kilkee, the train came to a shuddering halt and could not be moved. At an earlier stop in Ennistymon, weeds in the water that had been taken on board for the steam engine had clogged the engine. A furious French arrived at Moore's Hall more than five hours later, at 8.20 p.m. to find that most of his audience had already left. He sued West Clare Railway for loss of earnings and was awarded £10. On hearing that the passengers of the West Clare Railway were used to such delays, he wrote a song about the experience, and 'Are you right there Michael?' became one of his most successful songs. Management at the West Clare Railway Company were not amused and they took a libel case against the songwriter. On the morning of the hearing in Ennis Courthouse, French arrived late. When the judge asked him to explain his tardiness, he replied, 'Your Honour, I travelled by the West Clare Railway.' The court case was thrown out.

The West Clare railway line was opened on 2 July 1887. Two years earlier, Charles Stewart Parnell had turned the first sod at Miltown Malbay, using a silver spade that is now exhibited in the Clare County Museum in Ennis. It was a 3ft, narrow-gauge line and ran from Ennis via Ennistymon, Miltown Malbay, Lahinch, Kilkee and Kilrush. It transformed the lives of those living along the route as postal services improved and for the first time people had access to a daily newspaper. Tourists arrived to stay in the coastal town and to partake in festivals such as the Kilrush Horse Fair, Lahinch Garland Festival and Lisdoonvarna Festival. Cattle farmed on the Burren and other local produce were now easily transported from the region. By the turn of the century five trains a day were operating each way on the line, carrying an estimated 200,000 passengers annually and 80,000 tonnes of freight and livestock.

Diesel trains were brought into service in the late 1940s and the last steam train was withdrawn from the route in 1952. Throughout the 1950s the service ran at a loss and was closed for good in 1961. Expecting a huge crowd to take the last train, the West Clare Railway Company decided that the second last run of the service would be its last. Nonetheless, a large crowd gathered at Kilkee to watch as the train chugged into the station for the final time. They burst into song, singing, what else but, 'Are you right there Michael?'

KILKEE: A VICTORIAN SEASIDE RESORT

One of the most popular seaside resorts along the Wild Atlantic Way is Kilkee. Once a sleepy fishing village, its sheltered beach was a safe place from which to swim when sea bathing became popular at the end of the eighteenth century. Its popularity increased when the Napoleonic wars curtailed the Grand Tours of the sons of the landed gentry, and they came instead to Kilkee for their fun. In the 1820s villas and lodges were built for families to spend their summers by the coast. The locals opened businesses to service the influx of holidaymakers, providing some prosperity in an otherwise poor region. Soon anyone in possession of a donkey was offering rides on the beach to the children of Limerick day-trippers, who travelled down the

Shannon on steamboats. In the 1850s, Lord Conyngham, an absentee landlord, demolished the thatched mud cabin cottages of the original town to make way for more holiday homes. The extension of the West Clare Railway to Kilkee in 1892 made the town even more accessible to visitors. By then it was known as the 'Brighton of the West'.

A number of well-known Victorians visited the town in its heyday. The English poet Alfred Lord Tennyson visited twice in the 1840s with his friend Sir Aubrey De Vere of Curragh Chase House in Co. Limerick. He visited again in 1878 with members of his family, travelling from Limerick by steamer and staying in Moore's Hotel.

Another famous Victorian to visit Kilkee was Charlotte Brontë, the English author of *Jane Eyre*, who travelled there for her honeymoon. She married Arthur Bell Nichols, a curate in her father's parish of Haworth, in the Yorkshire Moors, on 29 June 1854. Their honeymoon took them first to Wales, where they boarded a steam packet at Holyhead bound for Dublin. Arthur Bell Nichols was born in Co. Antrim, but grew up in Banagher, Co. Offaly, with his uncle's family. The newlyweds spent some time in Banagher, where Arthur's brother was the manager of the Grand Canal Company. They then travelled along the shores of the Shannon to Limerick and then on to Kilkee, where they stayed at the West End Hotel run by a Mrs Shannon. In a letter to her former teacher, Catherine Wooler, Charlotte described the Atlantic as 'bold and grand'. However, she suggested in the same letter that Mrs Shannon's establishment had its 'shortcomings'. Other letters indicate that she and Arthur walked the cliffs near Kilkee and were enthralled by the views of the Atlantic Ocean. The remainder of their time in Ireland was spent in Tralee, Glengarriff and Killarney, where she fell from a horse while riding through the

Gap of Dunloe. Nine months later, in March 1855, Charlotte Brontë died.

Over a century later, Kilkee welcomed another well-known visitor. In September 1962, Che Guevara spent a night in Kilkee when his intended flight from Shannon was cancelled due to fog. In a pub that night he met the young Irish artist Jim Fitzpatrick, who served Che a drink in the Marine Hotel bar. In 1968, Fitzpatrick designed the iconic poster VIVA CHE, which he based on a photograph of the Cuban revolutionary that had been taken by Alberto Corda.

CLIFFS OF MOHER: CORNELIUS O'BRIEN

As the road rises from Liscannor towards the Cliffs of Moher, a column can be seen on a hill in the distance. O'Brien's Monument is a fine 24m Doric column topped with a carved stone urn, sitting on a square plinth. It commemorates the nineteenth-century landlord Cornelius O'Brien, who lived at the nearby Birchfield estate, and it was erected between 1858 and 1859, although the date inscribed on the plaque is 1853. The mason's error led to an accusation that O'Brien, who died in 1857, had the monument constructed in his lifetime with money 'wrung' from his tenants, or so wrote one journalist of the time. To further sully his reputation, legend had it that O'Brien fathered 100 children in the locality. The reality is rather different: O'Brien's tenants willingly contributed £36 for the memorial to a benevolent landlord.

Cornelius was born in about 1782 into the noble O'Brien family, descendants of Brian Boru, High King of Ireland. After studying at the King's Inn to be a lawyer, he dedicated his life to public service, becoming a magistrate for Co. Clare. In 1828 he was chairman of the election committee that selected Daniel

O'Connell as a candidate for the constituency. O'Connell's win led to the Catholic Emancipation Act of 1829. He was himself elected to the House of Commons as a Liberal MP in 1832, supporting O'Connell in his movement to have the 1800 Act of Union Act repealed. Cornelius O'Brien held the seat for Co. Clare until 1847, losing it in the election of that year, only to be re-elected five years later. Advancing age and ill health forced his retirement from parliament in March 1857, two months before his death.

He owned over 3,600 hectares of land in Co. Clare but, contrary to later accounts, O'Brien was a benevolent landlord, and while it is not documented, he possibly waived the rents of some of his tenants during the Famine. Travellers to the area in the post-Famine years commented on the neat, whitewashed cottages of the district, comparing them to the hovels they had witnessed in parts of Connemara. He provided work for his tenants by creating building projects, such as O'Brien's Bridge, between Lahinch and Liscannor, which dates from 1833. In this part of Co. Clare it is often said that the only thing O'Brien did not build was the Cliffs of Moher.

He was also responsible for the first pathway along the cliff edge, providing a viewing point from where the breathtaking views could be enjoyed. On 5 October 1854, an article in the *Clare Journal* written by 'an English Visitor' heaped praise on O'Brien for his developments at the Cliffs of Moher – the tower, pathways, stables, round picnic table and even the provision of a piper to entertain the visitors. In 2019, 1.6 million visitors walked the paths originally laid down by Cornelius O'Brien.

LISCANNOR: JOHN HOLLAND

John Holland was born in 1841 in Liscannor, where his father worked for the coast guard service. Apart from a younger brother, Holland's family survived the ravages of the Famine but the death of his father in 1853 saw the family move to Limerick. On finishing school, Holland joined the Christian Brothers order, moving between Limerick, Dublin, Dundalk and Cork while preparing to take his vows. In the North Monastery, Cork, he was encouraged to pursue his interest in engineering by Brother Dominic Burke. Among the projects he began working on was a design for a vessel that could travel underwater. He was also trying to design a flying machine. When Jules Verne published *20,000 Leagues Under the Sea* in 1870, Holland made it his life's ambition to turn the fantasy of underwater travel into a reality.

Due to ill health, he did not take his vows with the Christian brothers and left Ireland to go to America in 1873. In Boston, a broken leg allowed him time to work on his earlier design for a submarine.

His brother Michael had also emigrated to America and was involved with the Irish Republican Brotherhood and the Fenian movement there. He introduced his inventive brother to James Devoy and Jeremiah O'Donovan Rossa, the leading figures of the American Fenian movement. When they heard about Holland's designs for a submarine, they promised him funds to build what they saw as a potentially powerful weapon in their fight against the British. They gave him $4,000, which they collected from Irish emigrants who supported the Fenians in their efforts to gain Irish independence.

By June 1878, the Holland I was ready for a trial. It was built in Paterson, New Jersey, and was brought to the banks of the Passaic River, where, in front of a gathered crowd, it sank. The following day, after making adjustments, Holland's vessel was successfully submerged, travelled 365m and then resurfaced. Holland had built a working submarine.

Excited by this success, the Fenians pledged more money for the building of a bigger submarine. Holland II was called the 'Fenian Ram' by an American journalist and the name stuck. At 9m, it was twice as long as Holland I and could accommodate three people. Soon a third submarine was under construction. However, relations between Holland and the Fenian leadership soured when they threatened to sue him for an overrun on costs. By then Holland's interests were elsewhere.

The US Navy ran a competition for a viable submarine design, which Holland entered and won. Soon he was working on a new vessel, The Plunger, in Baltimore. As Holland did not have complete control of the project there were problems. The Navy insisted that he use a steam engine because all naval ships used them, but Holland knew it would not be suitable for a submarine. This led Holland to start a private venture, building the submarine that he thought would be best suited for naval use. It had an internal combustion engine for diving and resurfacing and an electric engine to propel the vessel when submerged. At a dockyard in Elizabethport, New Jersey, in 1896, the Holland VI was launched. After observing trials near Staten Island on 17 March 1898, the US Navy decided to buy the submarine and placed an order. Holland VI would become the standard design for submarines.

The US Naval Submarine division came into existence in 1900, when they took delivery of the first of Holland's submarines. Soon orders from other naval services followed: Japan, Russia, the Netherlands and eventually Great Britain. John Holland died on 12 August 1914 in Newark. Less than a month later, on 5 September 1914, HMS *Pathfinder* became the first ship to be sunk by a torpedo fired from a submarine.

FINAVARRA: THE MARTELLO TOWER, A NINETEENTH CENTURY COASTAL DEFENCE

Travelling from Ballyvaughan to Kinvara along the shore of Galway Bay, a small tower can be seen on a headland. This short, sturdy structure at Finavarra is one of approximately fifty Martello towers built around the Irish coast, between 1804 and 1810. The Martello tower on Garinish Island in Bantry Bay was the first in Ireland. The Finavarra tower is one of three on Galway Bay.

In 1793, France declared war on Great Britain and Ireland. The United Irishmen saw the war as an opportunity in their campaign for an Irish republic and petitioned the French for assistance in staging rebellions against British rule in Ireland. In 1796, and again in 1798, the French sent ships and soldiers to invade Ireland, each attempt being thwarted, most notably in Bantry Bay in 1796 by the Atlantic weather. However, the British Government were now alert to the fact that Ireland was vulnerable to invasion from their arch enemy. Coastal defences would have to be built.

During the war, in 1794, the Royal Navy came to the assistance of Corsican insurgents who were rising against the French. At Cape Martella, the Navy launched an attack on a French-held watchtower but after more than two hours of bombardment they had made no impact on the sturdy structure. The thick, curved walls of the tower meant that cannonballs just bounced right off. When a land force of 1,700 soldiers came ashore, it took them another two hours to capture the tower, which was manned by just thirty-three French soldiers operating just three cannon. When it came to protecting their own shores from a possible French attack, the British decided to use a similar structure, calling it a 'Martello Tower'.

The Martello towers of Galway Bay are at Rossaveal on the north side of the bay, and at Aughinish Island, and Finavarra to the south. Of the three, Finavarra is the most accessible. While some, such as the one at Garinish, are circular, the Finavarra tower is unusual in that it is an ovoid shape. All towers were built from cut stone and accessed by an external wooden stairs leading to a door on the first floor. The ground floor was the magazine where gunpowder was stored, above which were the living quarters. Cannon were placed on the roof, ready to open fire on any French ship entering the bay. The ruined building beside the Finavarra Martello tower was additional living quarters for the thirty or so soldiers posted there. The threat of French invasion receded when Napoleon was defeated at the Battle of Waterloo in 1815. Built to be indestructible, by the time they were abandoned no shot was ever fired in anger from any of the Martello towers and they were never bombarded. Today they stand intact, just as they were built.

5

COUNTY GALWAY

DOORUS: THE BEGINNINGS OF THE
IRISH LITERARY THEATRE

Coole Park, near Gort, home of Lady Augusta Gregory, is the spiritual home of the Irish literary renaissance, which made household names of Irish playwrights such as Yeats, Synge and O'Casey in the early twentieth century. However, the seeds for what became the Irish Literary Revival and would lead to the foundation of the Abbey Theatre were planted, not in the stately home of Coole Park, but in a more humble setting on the Co. Galway coastline.

Doorus House, near Kinvara, was the summer home of Count Florimonde de Basterot. He and Lady Gregory, whose summer home, Mount Vernon, was close by, often met to chat about literary trends in London, Paris and Rome. One July day in 1897, while Lady Gregory was visiting the Count, his cousin, Edward Martyn, arrived to discuss a business matter. Martyn's home, Tulira Castle, was close to Coole Park and he knew Lady Gregory well. With him was his own guest, William Butler Yeats. Yeats and Lady Gregory had met a few times prior to this, so while Martyn and the Count dealt with their business, Lady Gregory and Yeats took tea in the caretaker's office. There the conversation inevitably turned to literature. Yeats told Lady Gregory that he had written a play, *The Countess Cathleen*, which was ready for staging. When Martyn, also a playwright, and the Count joined their guests, they began discussing the need for an Irish theatre where Irish plays, written by Irish playwrights, could be performed. They wondered if an Irish audience would come to such a theatre.

Earlier in the decade, the Gaelic League had been founded and was promoting the revival of the Irish language. By drawing on the Celtic traditions of language, storytelling and art, a new Irish identity was being crafted to match the nationalist political mood of the day. Those gathered at Dorus House that day spent the rest of the afternoon making plans for a new Irish literary movement, the Irish Literary Revival. At the heart of that plan was a new theatre company, initially called the Celtic Theatre but later the Irish National Theatre.

For the rest of that summer, Yeats stayed with Lady Gregory at Coole Park. She drew up a list of wealthy people who could be petitioned for funding. Possible guarantors were informed that each spring the theatre would produce a series of Irish or Celtic plays in Dublin. The plays intended to portray Ireland not as the 'home of buffoonery' but the home of 'an ancient idealism'. They believed Ireland had an 'uncorrupted' audience and were confident that Irish audiences would embrace the experience.

Between them, Lady Gregory, Martyn and Yeats had the plays and the funding for a theatre. However, regulations in Dublin did not allow for setting up a new one. Conveniently, in 1898, a change to the Local Government Bill allowed Dublin County Council to grant an occasional licence for performances. The first production of the Irish Literary Theatre was staged on 8 May 1899 at the Antient Concert Rooms on Great Brunswick Street (now Pearse Street) in Dublin. Yeats's *The Countess Cathleen* was performed and well received. The second night was even more successful, with Edward Martyn's *The Heather Field* receiving rave reviews. The following year the Company staged plays by Martyn and George Moore at the Gaiety Theatre. By 1901, money was scarce and lack of public interest led to it being the last season of the Irish Literary Theatre.

However, that plan, hatched on the Atlantic coast at Doorus House, did not end there. In 1903, Lady Gregory, Yeats and John Millington Synge secured funding for the Irish National Theatre Society. They also joined forces with Frank and William Fay, who had their own company of Irish acting talent. A lease was taken out on the Mechanic Theatre on Abbey Street and on 27 December 1904, Yeats's plays *On Baile's Strand* and *Cathleen Ní Houlihan*, and Lady Gregory's *Spreading the News* were performed by the theatre company that would forever more be known as the Abbey Theatre.

KINVARA: THE OWNERS OF DUNGUAIRE CASTLE

Before there was ever a castle on this little inlet of Galway Bay, outside Kinvara, the seventh-century Gúaire, King of Connacht, had a 'dún' or a 'fort' here. He was a cousin of the pious St Colman, who had built the nearby monastery of Kilmacduagh. St Colman badgered Gúaire regularly to be more generous to the poor, but his pleas fell on deaf ears. Legend has it that one day, as Gúaire sat down to enjoy a particularly sumptuous banquet, the plates, laden with food, suddenly rose from the table and flew out the window. Gúaire ran outside, saddled up his horse and followed the flying plates. They brought him to Kilmacduagh, where he found St Colman distributing the food to the needy.

The castle, which dates from about 1520, is a tower keep surrounded by an irregular-shaped 'bawn', the Irish term for a

defensive wall. It was built by Murtogh O'Heyne, a descendant of Guaire's, and a member of a Gaelic clan dominant in south Galway until the 1600s. In 1594, Aedh O'Heyne, under Queen Elizabeth I's policy of 'Surrender and Regrant', pledged allegiance to the Crown and was allowed to retain his south Galway lands. However, by supporting the Gaelic Lords during the Nine Years' War, he fell out of favour and by 1615 Dunguaire was in the ownership of Oliver Martyn. His descendant, Richard Martyn, Mayor of Galway in 1642, lived at the castle, which remained in that family until the twentieth century.

The last Martyn to own Dunguaire Castle was Edward Martyn of Tulira Castle. When he heard that his friend William Butler Yeats was looking for a home in Co. Galway, he offered it to him. However, by then Dunguaire was roofless and not fit for habitation. Yeats, wisely, declined the offer, instead buying Thor Ballylee near Gort. Martyn eventually sold the castle to Oliver St John Gogarty for £90. Gogarty was a Dublin surgeon, writer and Nationalist. He extracted William Butler Yeats's tonsils and was the doctor who performed the autopsy on Michael Collins when he was killed in 1922. He features as Buck Mulligan in James Joyce's *Ulysses*. Gogarty was a witty poet but decided to turn his hand to writing a novel to fund the refurbishment of the derelict castle. He intended using the royalties from *As I Was Walking Down Sackville Street* to convert Dunguaire into a country retreat. However, the book did not sell well and he only managed to put a roof on the building.

In the 1950s, in need of funds, Gogarty sold Dunguaire to Lady Christobel Ampthill, a keen fox-hunting English aristocrat, who refurbished the castle and lived there until her death in 1976. She endeared herself to the local community and hunted regularly with the Galway Blazers Hunt, always riding side-saddle.

Lady Ampthill had been embroiled in a sensational scandal in London during the 1920s. In 1918 she married John Russell, later Lord Ampthill. The couple did not want children but, in 1921, she discovered she was pregnant, even though the couple had not consummated their marriage. At the insistence of his family, Russell filed for divorce, accusing Christobel of adultery, which she denied. During the ensuing court case, and the numerous appeals that followed, the London press lapped up the proceedings and particularly relished the evidence that after a medical examination, the pregnant Christobel was, in fact, found to be a virgin. Her son, Geoffrey, had been born by then, leading to headlines proclaiming his arrival as 'the Virgin Birth'. One lawyer suggested that the pregnancy had occurred after Christobel had used the same bath sponge as her husband.

In 1924, the case was appealed to the House of Lords, who decided that, since Geoffrey was born in wedlock, he should be legitimised as Lord Ampthill's heir. The couple eventually divorced in 1937.

After years of living quietly at Dunguaire, the story of her son's paternity came into the news again following the death of her ex-husband in 1973. Geoffrey's right to his father's title was challenged by his stepbrother but the House of Lords' decision of 1924 was upheld. Sadly, Christabel died, aged 80, without knowing the verdict. Today Dunguaire Castle is run as a heritage site.

GALWAY: THE CITY OF THE TRIBES

Turlough O'Connor, the King of Connacht, was the first to make a settlement at the mouth of the Gallamh river. In 1124 he built Bun Gallamh on the west shore of the fast-flowing river, named after Gallamh, the daughter of King Breslin, who fell into the rapids and was swept into the bay, never to be seen again. In the nineteenth century the river was renamed the Corrib. At 6km, it is the shortest river in Europe.

In 1171, King Henry II declared himself Lord of Ireland and granted swathes of land to Anglo-Norman nobles who came to Ireland with him. It would be another fifty years before they crossed the Shannon into Connacht. That charge was led by Richard de Burgo, newly created Lord of Connacht, who reached the west coast in 1234, where he built a settlement on the east shore of the Gallamh. The Gaelic O'Connor and O'Flaherty chieftains took none too kindly to the interlopers and burnt them out, whereupon de Burgo returned in 1236 with reinforcements. By the 1270s, his grandson, the Red Earl, had built a castle and a sturdy wall around the town of Galway.

For the next 300 years, the town-dwelling Anglo-Normans lived behind the defensive walls, while the Gaelic families were excluded from the town. In 1518 Galway officials passed a statute banning any family whose name began with 'O' or 'Mac' from the streets of Galway. By then this law applied to the de Burgos, who, like many Anglo-Normans, had become more Irish than the Irish themselves. Their name was now Burke and by the late fourteenth century they had lost control of the walled town their ancestors had founded.

Filling the power vacuum were fourteen gentrified merchant families, who transformed Galway into a thriving seaport in the 1400s. Athy, Blake, Browne, Bodkin, D'Arcy, Deane, French, Font, Joyce, Kirwan, Lynch, Martin, Morris and Skerrett were the names of the fourteen families, who between them built a harbour and established trade links with Bristol, London, Orkney, Amsterdam, St Malo, Nantes, La Rochelle, Bordeaux, Lisbon, and Seville.

They exported animal hides, wool, cloth, tallow and salted fish, and imported iron and salt, but also luxuries such as wine, spices and silks. By the sixteenth century, they were trading with the Gaelic lords outside the walls, buying turf and sheep from Connemara. The pinnacle of these merchant family's achievements came when, in 1484, King Richard III granted Galway a city charter.

Marriages between the families and shared business interests had created a tight-knit community. Sir Thomas Blake, who lived in Galway in the seventeenth century, married three times – firstly to a Martin, then a Lynch and finally a French. Oliver Cromwell stormed into Ireland in 1649 and changed the fortunes of the fourteen merchant families forever. His soldiers dubbed them 'the Tribes of Galway'; they were not being complimentary. Cromwell famously ordered the Irish Catholics to go 'to Hell or to Connacht'. He confiscated the lands and wealth of families who clung to their Catholic faith and banished them to the poor land, west of the Shannon. This order also applied to the Catholic 'Tribes'. Many lost all they had, while others, such as the thrice-married Sir Thomas Blake, gave into Cromwell's demands and to preserve their wealth they converted to Protestantism.

The final blow to the Tribes of Galway came after the Battle of Aughrim in 1691. Those families who had managed to retain their commercial interests, despite remaining Catholic, felt the full force of the Penal Laws imposed on Catholics by King William III. They were no longer allowed to trade or hold positions of power. Many fled with the Wild Geese to the Continent, while others turned their hand to smuggling goods on their previously established trade routes. By the eighteenth century, new families such as the Eyres were the power-brokers of Galway.

Of the 'Tribes', the Lynch family left the most lasting legacy. They commissioned St Nicholas Collegiate church and their townhouse, Lynch's Castle, stands proudly in the commercial centre of Galway to this day. It was a Lynch who successfully petitioned King Richard III for the grant of a city charter in 1484. Persse Lynch Fitzjohn became the first Mayor of the new city in 1485, the first of eighty-four Lynches who would hold the title up to 1654.

Galway's most famous story involves the Lynch family. One version tells how James Lynch Fitzstephen, the Mayor of Galway in the 1490s, sent his son, Walter, to Spain to bring home a cargo of wine. Walter spent most of the money for the transaction at ports along the way. In Spain, and with no money, he managed to persuade the Spanish merchant to send his nephew, Gomez, to Galway with Walter, where he promised that his father would pay for the cargo of wine. However, Gomez never made it to Galway as Walter murdered him on the voyage home, disposing of his body in the ocean. Walter's father only came to learn of the terrible deed when one of the crew from the voyage spoke of the murder on his deathbed. Trade between the two ports could not be jeopardised, so justice had to be served. Walter was tried and found guilty of murder. In the fifteenth century the penalty for murder was death by hanging. However, nobody was willing to hang the Mayor's son, so James Lynch Fitzstephen had to hang his own son for the murder.

Another family of note were the Martins, who were the first of the Tribes to venture beyond the protection of the city walls. In the 1600s they bought lands in Connemara from the O'Flahertys. They almost lost these gains when Richard 'Nimble Dick' Martin sided with the losing Jacobites during the Williamite–Jacobite war of the early 1690s. He visited King William III in London to plead his case. His 'nimble' powers of persuasion convinced the King that Martin should keep his Galway estate, thus gaining him his nickname. The most famous of the Martins is Richard 'Humanity Dick' Martin, the great grandson of Nimble Dick. He founded the Royal Society for Prevention of Cruelty to Animals in 1822. He once boasted to his friend, King George IV, that the avenue to his home at Ballynahinch Castle stretched from Galway, a distance of 64 km, and was longer than the King's avenue to Windsor Castle.

In more recent years a member of the Morris family achieved global recognition. Michael Morris, 3rd Baron Killanin, was President of the International Olympic Committee between 1972 and 1980, serving two terms, during which he oversaw the hostage situation during the Munich Games and the boycotts of the Moscow Games.

Today, Galway embraces the legacy of these fourteen medieval merchant families, as it proudly calls itself 'the City of the Tribes'.

THREE ST NICHOLAS'S CHURCHES IN GALWAY

Two churches are prominent on the Galway skyline, one has a spire and the other has a copper dome. Both are dedicated to St Nicholas of Myra, more commonly known as the patron saint of children or Santa Claus, but also the patron saint of mariners. There is a 600-year age difference between the two churches and, in the intervening years, a third St Nicholas church also catered for the faithful of Galway.

The oldest of the churches is St Nicholas' Collegiate Church in the heart of Galway. Built in 1320 inside the town walls, its landmark spire was added in the 1680s and the three clocks in 1898. In the fifteenth century, the Lynch and French families funded the building of two new aisles on either side of the original nave. This gave the church its unusual three-gabled west facade. This is how it would have looked to Christopher Columbus when he came to pray there on a visit to Galway in 1477.

The interior of St Nicholas has all the hallmarks of a medieval church: a sixteenth-century baptismal font that is still in use, an apprentice's pillar and a knight's tomb. The benefactors of the church are also well represented, with the Lynch Memorial Window tomb, bearing their coat of arms, and the Lynch Flamboyant Altar tomb, all in the south transept. Many of the carvings on these tombs are defaced, a legacy of Cromwell's soldiers who, in addition to vandalising the church, also stabled their horses inside it.

St Nicholas Church was originally a Catholic parish church in the diocese of Tuam. When Galway was granted city status in 1484, the governors of the new city appealed to Pope Innocent VIII for control of their own church. He designated St Nicholas's a collegiate church, giving the newly established City Corporation the power to appoint a warden and eight vicars to administer it. During the reign of King Edward VI the church was taken over by the Protestant community. It reverted briefly to Catholicism before Cromwell arrived, and again, during the Williamite–Jacobite war of the 1690s. Since then St Nicholas's has been a place of worship for the Anglican parishioners of Galway and is the oldest parish church in continuous use in Ireland.

In 1816, the Protestant Mayor of Galway, Hyacinth Daly, laid the foundation stone for St Nicholas's Roman Catholic Church on the corner of Abbeygate Street and Middle Street. The Penal Laws, although still in existence, had been relaxed and the Catholic community of Galway once again had a parish church in which to worship. Daniel O'Connell, the architect of the Catholic Emancipation, attended mass in the church on St Patrick's Day, 1841.

In 1831, the Catholic Diocese of Galway was created. A diocese needs a cathedral, but in the absence of funds to build a new cathedral, the existing parish church of St Nicholas became the pro-cathedral for Galway. By 1876, plans were underway for a new, permanent cathedral but progress was painstakingly slow and St Nicholas Pro-Cathedral would serve the Catholics of Galway for another ninety years before it was deconsecrated, sold and converted into offices.

By 1909, Bishop McCormack had raised enough money to buy an old military barracks at O'Brien's Bridge in the city. However, by the 1930s, Bishop Michael Browne was advised that the site was no longer suitable for a church. Times had changed, a bigger church was needed and the O'Brien's Bridge site would not have any room for car parking. Forty years after the purchase of the original site, a new, more suitable one became available. The Government of the day planned to demolish Galway's Old Jail, which was located across the

Salmon Weir Bridge from the Court House. The land was transferred to the Bishop of Galway to build a new cathedral. It did not escape Galwegians' notice that the use of the site was being transferred from sinners to saints!

The outbreak of the Second World War led to further delays. Cardinal D'Alton finally laid the foundation stone on 27 October 1957 at a ceremony attended by bishops from all over Ireland, the President of Ireland, Sean T. O'Kelly and the Taoiseach, John A. Costello. Pope Pius XII personally approved the plans of Dublin architect John J. Robinson. Sisk and Co. Ltd was contracted to build the church for £600,000. On 14 August 1965, Cardinal Cushing of Boston said the first Mass in the new cathedral. The following day, on the Feast of the Assumption, the cathedral was dedicated to Our Lady Assumed into Heaven and St Nicholas of Myra.

St Nicholas Chapel in the cathedral holds a link between all three St Nicholas churches of Galway. Embedded in the wall is a stone triptych of carved figures representing Our Blessed Lady, and the Blessed Trinity. The carvings are seventeenth

century in origin, and were originally located in the vestry of St Nicholas' Collegiate Church. In the late eighteenth century, the Protestant warden had them removed and ordered that they be thrown into the sea. A Catholic priest met the carter tasked with the disposal of the triptych and persuaded him to bring them, instead, to the Catholic parish church, which later became the pro-cathedral. They were placed on a wall there until they were again moved in the 1960s, this time to the new cathedral, from where they continue to watch over Galway's faithful.

THE GALWAY LINE

On 1 August 1851, the first train pulled into the newly opened Galway railway station. With Dublin now just four hours away, plans were being made to operate transatlantic passenger liners from Galway. Interestingly, the driving force behind this project was a local priest, Fr Peter Daly.

Fr Daly was a charismatic cleric who held positions on the boards of the Town Commissioners, the Gas Company and the Harbour Commissioners. However, his involvement in Galway's civic affairs did not sit well with his clerical superiors, and he was often embroiled in controversy. As a young clergyman, he famously argued with a Protestant minister over the faith of a Galway man lying on his deathbed. Fr Daly's hopes of becoming the first bishop of the new diocese of Galway were dashed when he received just one vote in the election. Some of his fellow priests suggested that he had voted for himself.

Nonetheless, he worked tirelessly for the betterment of Galway. In 1858, with John Orrel Lever, a Manchester shipping line owner, Fr Daly set up the Atlantic Royal Mail Steam Navigation Company, raising money by selling shares in the new venture. They leased a wooden-hulled sail ship, *Indian Empire*, for the first transatlantic crossing. On 16 June, the ship arrived at the mouth of Galway Bay, where two local pilots were taken onboard to bring the ship to Galway harbour. The only hazard in the 15-km-wide channel of Galway Bay is the Margaretta Rock, named after the naval vessel that fell afoul of it in 1807. However, Henry Burbridge and Patrick Wallace, two experienced pilots, managed to ground the *Indian Empire* on the rock.

An enquiry that very afternoon attended by Fr Daly found the two pilots negligent in their duty and both were arrested. The local newspapers were full of conspiracy theories, suggesting that the pilots had been bribed by parties interested in scuppering the fledgling shipping line. The finger of suspicion was pointed at shipping businesses in Liverpool, where the Galway Line was seen as a threat to their monopoly on the transatlantic passenger business from the British Isles. The conspiracy theorists went into overdrive when, while out on bail and awaiting trial, Patrick Wallace was found dead. Even though the official cause of death was recorded as natural causes, rumours persisted. This story gets a mention in James Joyce's *Ulysses*, published many years later.

The future of the Galway Line looked certain when, in 1860, it was awarded the contract to carry the Royal Mail from Galway to North America. Conditions in the contract stipulated that penalties would be charged for late delivery of mail. By then, the company had commissioned four iron-hulled paddle steamers, rigged with sails, the first of which, *Connaught*, was launched in Jarrow, England, in April 1860. Her maiden voyage left Galway for New York on 26 June 1860. However, *Connaught* did not leave Connaught, as before the ship even got to the mouth of Galway Bay, a mechanical fault brought her to a halt.

The next voyage was scheduled for 11 July and this time the *Connaught* was heading for Boston via St John's in Newfoundland. Nineteen hours into the sailing, once again her engines let her down and she limped into St John's, eventually reaching Boston two days late. The same mechanical issues plagued the *Connaught* on the return leg to Galway. Management at the Galway Line were worried about the impact these delays would have on the lucrative mail contract. After major mechanical repairs and sea trials, by September, *Connaught* was once again Boston bound. Captain Robert Leitch was at the helm of the ship, which was carrying fifty-seven first-class passengers, 396 steerage passengers, 124 crew, £10,000 in gold and the all-important mail. But en route to Newfoundland, the ship encountered such fierce weather that on reaching St John's, Fr Peter Conway, the parish priest of Headford, disembarked. He and some other passengers were so frightened that they refused to continue to Boston.

Nonetheless, *Connaught* left St John's, but 150 miles from Boston, Captain Leitch was informed that water was spilling into the engine room. Soon the furnaces were swamped with water, quenching the fires, which led to the engines shutting down. Smoke was seen coming from the hold, and before long the lower part of the ship was in flames. Fortunately, Captain Wilson on the *Minnie Schiffer*, a small American cargo ship, saw the distress signals and came to the assistance of the stricken *Connaught*. Over the course of two and half hours, passengers were winched to lifeboats and then on to the small cargo ship. All passengers and crew were rescued. The last to leave the blazing *Connaught* was Captain Leitch. The *Minnie Schiffer* arrived in Boston to much acclaim, and Captain Wilson was declared the hero of the hour. No lives were lost, but the *Connaught*, all her cargo and mail sank to the bottom of the Atlantic.

The Galway Line ceased operating in 1864. Of the Galway Line's founders, John Orrel Lever was declared bankrupt, and as Fr Daly had also fallen foul of the Bishop, for neglect of his clerical duties, his involvement in public affairs was thereafter curtailed.

GALWAY TIME

Until 1916, Dublin's time was officially twenty-five minutes and twenty-one seconds behind London, having been determined by the local time at the Dunsink Observatory. Going further west, the time continued to change, and so Galway Time was another eleven and a half minutes behind Dublin Mean Time. Different parts of the country on different times did not have any real impact until the arrival of the railway. Companies operating timetabled services needed a standard time, and so Dublin Mean Time was used.

However, many western towns, including Galway, continued to operate eleven and a half minutes behind Dublin Mean Time and kept public clocks on local time. One newspaper reported, in 1870, that a troop of soldiers, making their way home for Christmas, missed their train from Galway because they had used the local town clock, which was on Galway time. If their train was timetabled for 11 a.m. Dublin Mean Time, but they arrived at 11 a.m. Galway Time, then the train was already eleven and a half minutes on its way to Dublin.

In 1880, Dublin Mean Time was officially applied throughout Ireland. However, some publicans in Galway were known to use the excuse that they were still on Galway Time if patrons were found on the premises just after closing time! In October 1916, the Time (Ireland) Act was passed in Westminster, bringing all of Ireland into Greenwich Mean Time, which meant the entire nation lost twenty-five minutes that October.

SCREEBE: THE LADY DUDLEY NURSES

Lady Rachel Dudley was the wife of William Ward, 2nd Earl Dudley, who served as the Lord Lieutenant of Ireland between 1902 and 1905. On a visit to Inver Lodge, in Connemara, she was shocked by the poverty in the region. She found it particularly disturbing that the poor had no access to doctors or any kind of medical care. Using her position as wife of the Lord Lieutenant, she began lobbying the Congested District Board, politicians and landowners for funding to provide a medical service, initially in Connemara but later in other remote regions along the Atlantic seaboard. The first nurse employed under the Dudley Scheme began working in the Bealadangan area of Connemara in 1903. The nurses were provided with a cottage, a bicycle and medical supplies. The bicycles were of little use as there were few roads. Initially, the Dudley nurses were met with suspicion as many were Protestant and did not speak Irish. They also came up against superstitions and an unwillingness by their patients to leave behind the traditional folk remedies, passed from mother to daughter, and embrace science-based medicine. These pioneering women dealt with every conceivable ailment, from broken bones and confinements, to infectious diseases. Although sixty years since the Potato Famine, their clientele were still undernourished and living in cottages with no sanitation and poor ventilation: conditions that often contributed to their illnesses. The nurses worked all year round, providing a health service that had never existed before. In 1913, it was decided that a nurse would only spend three years in the service, such was the toll it took on their health.

When Lady Dudley's husband was sent to Australia as Governor-General, she began fundraising for a similar service in the Australian outback, which would later become the Flying Doctor Service. During the First World War, after much opposition, she opened a hospital in northern France to cater for wounded soldiers.

Connemara had made an impression on Lady Dudley, and after the war she continued to visit. By then she was divorced from her husband, who had left her for a music hall actress. She always stayed at Screebe House, in Room 4. In the summer of 1920 she was once again visiting Connemara. While swimming in the sea near Screebe, she tragically drowned. Her legacy continued with her friend, Lady Mayo, collecting £40,000 in funding for the service in the year following her death. The nursing service that she provided saved thousands of lives and remained in existence until the 1970s, when it was absorbed into the state-funded Regional Health Boards.

ROSMUC: PEARSE'S COTTAGE

Hidden in trees overlooking Lough Arrolagh outside the village of Rosmuc in Connemara is a small thatched cottage, which is today a national monument. It belonged to Padraig Pearse, the Commander-in-Chief of the 1916 Easter Rising. Pearse was born in Dublin in 1879 and during his childhood an elderly aunt filled his head with stories of Wolf Tone and the Fenians. He was educated by the Christian Brothers at Westland Row but, as Irish was not then part of the school curriculum, he began taking classes privately. He went on to study Law and Arts at the Royal University (later University College Dublin). He joined the Gaelic League in 1896 and he was soon an active member, writing articles for *An Claidheamh Soluis*, the organisation's newspaper, later becoming its editor between 1903 and 1909. He also taught

Irish. James Joyce attended some classes given by Pearse but found them and the teacher boring.

Pearse first came to Co. Galway in 1898, spending time on the Aran Islands improving his Irish among the native speakers. He came to love the Gaeltacht region of Connemara and became a regular visitor. In 1905 he visited Rosmuc, where he befriended the principal of the local school, Padraig O'Conghaile, who helped him secure a plot of land. He built the small thatched cottage as a place to write and get away from his busy career in Dublin.

He changed career in 1909, opening St Enda's School, where children were taught through Irish. Originally a supporter of the Home Rule movement, by 1913 Pearse's politics had become more radical. He envisaged an independent Ireland, where everyone spoke Irish and the language was taught in all the schools. More importantly, he believed that the only way of achieving independence was by a 'blood sacrifice': a rebellion. He joined the Irish Volunteers when they were founded in 1913, and was soon elected to the Supreme Council.

When the elderly Fenian Jeremiah O'Donovan Rossa died in 1915 the Irish Republican Brotherhood decided to use his funeral as a rallying cry to the Irish public, calling them to back a movement towards Irish independence. The IRB leader, Tom Clarke, decided that Pearse should write and deliver the graveside oration. When Pearse asked Clarke how far he should go with the speech, he was told to throw caution to the wind. After days in the tranquillity of Rosmuc, Pearse returned to Dublin with a speech that he did not show to anyone. He would never return to his cottage again.

On 1 August 1915, a procession of 20,000 people made up of Irish Volunteers, GAA teams, Gaelic societies and pipe bands followed the coffin of O'Donovan Rossa through the streets of Dublin. It was the biggest show of Irish Nationalism ever seen in Ireland. At the graveside in Glasnevin Cemetery, Pearse delivered the oration, which left the British in no doubt that a fervent Nationalist movement was stirring in Ireland. The call was for not only a Gaelic Ireland but an Ireland free from British rule.

Pearse would address the people of Ireland one more time in his short life. On the first day of the 1916 Easter Rising, under the portico of the GPO as Commander-in-Chief, he read the *Proclamation of the Irish Republic*, a document he had helped write. After a week of fighting, Pearse agreed to surrender to the British. He was executed in Kilmainham Gaol on 3 May 1916 for his part in the Rising. He knew that the Rising was doomed to fail, but hoped that his blood sacrifice would further the cause of Irish independence. The cottage in Rosmuc was inherited by his mother but was burned down by the Black and Tans in 1921. His sisters gave the property to the state in 1943.

CLIFDEN: MARCONI AND ALCOCK AND BROWN

Guglielmo Marconi, the Italian pioneer of wireless communication, was no stranger to Ireland. His mother was Annie Jameson, of the Irish whiskey family and his first wife was Beatrice O'Brien of Dromoland Castle. In 1901, his transatlantic wireless station at Poldhu in Cornwall was communicating with Newfoundland. He wanted another station further west, and in 1905 he found the perfect site just outside Clifden on the Derrygimlagh Bog.

There were several factors why the Clifden site was ideal for Marconi's station. To begin with, it offered a direct, uninterrupted line across the Atlantic to Nova Scotia, the nearest point of the American continent to Ireland. The heavy equipment needed for the project was conveniently landed at Clifden pier. The town had a rail connection to Galway and could supply a willing and able workforce. Finally, the Derrygimlagh Bog provided a ready source of fuel, needed for generating the electricity required for the operation.

The extensive buildings on the site included a boiler house, an electricity-generating hall, a transmission room and staff quarters. The most imposing structures were the eight, 60m-high transmission masts. The Clifden station began transmitting communications to Glace Bay in Nova Scotia on 17 October 1907. Once transmission began, the masts would have been alive with flying sparks, lighting up the night sky over the bog. At its peak, 350 people were employed at the Marconi station, the majority of them being seasonal workers employed to cut and gather turf. In 1922, during the Civil War, the station was burnt down. It closed permanently shortly afterwards, leaving the buildings to crumble.

One employee at the station was John George 'Jack' Phillips. From Godalming in England, he worked as a junior wireless operator on ships such as the *Teutonic* and the *Lusitania* before being sent to work at the Clifden station. In 1912 he was sent to Belfast to install equipment on the White Star Line's newest ship, *Titanic*. Philips was given the job of Senior Wireless Operator on the ship's maiden voyage. He sent the distress signal when *Titanic* struck an iceberg mid Atlantic and stayed at his post until the power on board failed. He did not survive the disaster.

An event that occurred at the Derrygimlagh Bog near the Marconi Station in 1919 could easily have ended in disaster. Instead, it turned into a record-breaking achievement for two aviators. In June of that year, sixteen years after the Wright Brothers had successfully made their first flight at Kitty Hawk, two intrepid aviators, Captain John Alcock and his navigator, Lieutenant Arthur Whitten Brown, took to the air in a Vickers Vimy biplane, intent on crossing the Atlantic Ocean. They aimed to pilot the first, non-stop flight across the Atlantic. They also hoped to win the £10,000 prize being offered by the *Daily Mail* newspaper to the first aviators to succeed. Both men were from Manchester and were experienced pilots, having served in the Royal Flying Corps during the First World War. They left from St John's in Newfoundland and after sixteen hours in the air, having covered 3,000 km, they saw the Irish coastline. Their immediate plan was to land the plane, preferably on a firm, flat piece of ground. They saw what looked like a suitable place near the town of Clifden. It might have looked suitable, but the Derrygimlagh Bog, where Alcock and Brown landed on 15 June 1919, was far from flat or firm. Fortunately only the plane was damaged in the bumpy landing. Word of their success was sent to London from the nearby Marconi Station. Alcock and Brown were given knighthoods and later collected the prize money, which was presented to them by Winston Churchill. Sadly, Alcock died in a flying accident that same year. Arthur Brown died in 1948.

There are two monuments near Clifden commemorating the remarkable achievement of Alcock and Brown. The first is a white cairn in the bog located near the actual landing site. The other monument is a sculpture of an aeroplane's tail fin on a hill overlooking the Derrygimlagh Bog, which was erected to commemorate the fortieth anniversary of the landing.

6

COUNTY MAYO

THE FAMINE IN COUNTY MAYO

The Famine of the 1840s left an indelible impact on Ireland. Between 1845 and 1849, the failure of the potato crop, the crop upon which the majority of the population depended, led to the death of 1 million people and the emigration of millions more. According to the 1841 Census, there were 65,000 tenant farmers, most with large families, in Co. Mayo, renting plots of just one acre from local and absentee landlords. On these plots the tenants planted potatoes, which grew well in the poor soil and provided a better yield than a cereal crop from the meagre plot. The authorities, however, referred to the potato fields as 'the Lazy Beds', implying that their tenants were too lazy to grow anything else.

The year 1845 looked like being a bumper one for the potato crop. However, hopes were dashed when the leaves began to wither and the tubers blackened and rotted in the ground. The damp, humid weather conditions of the summer were ideal for the spread of *Phytophthora infestans*, the Potato Blight. There followed years of devastation, as subsequent crops were also decimated by the blight. Those dependent on potatoes had no food, no money and eventually no homes, as landlords evicted them for non-payment of rent.

In Co. Mayo two of the biggest landowners, Sir Roger Palmer and Lord Lucan, who between them owned 57,000 hectares of the county, were particularly ruthless in clearing tenants off their lands. Tenants, often dying from starvation and the diseases that came with hunger, were turned out on to the roads, their cottages pulled down so they could not squat. If they had any money, the displaced tenants booked a passage and emigrated to America or Canada. For those with no money, the only option open to them was the workhouse.

In 1838, a system of Poor Relief was set up in Ireland. The country was divided into 130 Unions, each with a workhouse, which were funded from rates collected from landowners and businesses. There was no proper system for collecting rates, and the Unions that had the highest number of destitute people and, therefore, required the most funds, were often the ones with the lowest number of ratepayers. Landowners, such as Palmer and Lucan, were in arrears on their rates during the famine years, which meant the workhouses of Mayo were not properly funded. At the outbreak of the Famine, Westport workhouse did not have the funds to feed the 600 paupers already accommodated there. By November 1848, the workhouse was sheltering 1,800 people.

To gain entry to the workhouse, families had to be destitute and have no claim to land. By 1849, a system of Poor Relief was put in place to provide aid outside of the workhouses, which helped the majority who held plots of land, but who had no food. The Poor Relief system was, however, poorly funded and badly administered. This led to one of the most distressing episodes of the Famine years in Co. Mayo.

At the end of March 1849, Captain Primrose, a Poor Law inspector with the Westport Union, and Colonel Hogrove, a Guardian of the Westport Union, were tasked with assessing those in need of relief in the town of Louisburgh and the surrounding area. Crowds of people, desperately in need of food, arrived in the town to meet with the officials. Showing scant concern for their plight, the officials announced that they would assess each individual's eligibility the following morning, at seven o'clock at Delphi Lodge, some 16 km away.

Many in the crowd believed that they would be given food at Delphi, so almost 600 hungry men, women and children began the trek along the road that took them past Glenullin and Doolough Lakes, through Doolough Valley, in the lee of Mweelrea mountain. The cold, wet March weather made the journey even more arduous. At Delphi, the officials did not appear until midday and offered little by way of relief. Starving and further weakened by the long difficult walk, it was inevitable that some souls perished on the return trek. At least seven died on the side of the road, their bodies not found for days. Post-mortem examinations determined that they had died from starvation.

Today, the road through the Doolough Valley is known as the Famine Walk. This narrow winding road through a valley, bordered with lakes and having a steep incline towards Louisburgh is perfect west of Ireland scenery. Visible in the landscape is a legacy of those tenant farmers of the 1840s. The now overgrown ridges and furrows of the 'Lazy Beds' line the slopes of the hills. A memorial cross on the roadside at Lough Glenullin is a reminder of how desolate this landscape must have seemed to the 600 souls who walked it, in the hope of getting food in the spring of 1849. The inscription on the cross is a quote from Mahatma Gandhi that reads 'How can men feel themselves honoured by humiliation of their fellow beings?'

There are, however, also stories of landlords who almost bankrupted themselves trying to help their tenants during those desolate years. As Chairman of the Westport workhouse, John Browne, 3rd Marquess of Sligo, provided money to keep the workhouse going. Towards the latter years of the Famine, his only source of income came from hiring out a box the family held at the Royal Opera House in Covent Garden, London. Another Mayo landlord, George Henry Moore of Moore Hall, also helped his tenants. In 1846 his horse, Coranna, won the Chester Cup, scooping £10,000 in prize money. Moore reportedly said 'no tenant of mine shall want for plenty of everything this year'.

Census records show that the population of Co. Mayo fell by almost a third between 1841 and 1851. In 1997, to commemorate the 150th anniversary of 'Black '47', the worst year of the Famine, a National Famine Memorial was proposed. Because Co. Mayo was one of the worst-affected counties, it was decided to locate John Behan's poignant monument at Murrisk, at the foot of Croagh Patrick, on the shores of Clew Bay. Unveiled by then President of Ireland, Mary Robinson, a native of Ballina, the memorial depicts a masted coffin ship, with the rigging made from skeletal figures, and stands as a permanent reminder of the darkest years of Ireland's history.

ST PATRICK

Every year, on 17 March, the world celebrates with Ireland in commemorating its patron saint, St Patrick, who is credited with bringing Christianity to Ireland. The Eiffel Tower and other world monuments are illuminated green for the day, and in Ireland it is a day of parades. What is known about St Patrick is a mixture of fact and myth. Even though St Patrick was the first to use the written word in Ireland, leaving just two written documents, there is scant documentary evidence about him. Of the facts, one thing is certain, St Patrick was not Irish. He was born around AD 420, most likely in Wales, or possibly western Scotland. At the age of 16 he was kidnapped by Irish raiders, sold into slavery and for six years sat on the side of Slemish Mountain in Co. Antrim, tending sheep. While there, he turned to God for comfort, and when he eventually escaped, he went to Gaul (France) and became a Christian priest.

In his dreams he saw the Irish pagans imploring him to return and preach the Word of God. He returned in AD 432 to begin his mission. Ireland was never colonised by the Romans, but by the fifth century there were definite trade links between the south coast of Ireland and Roman Britain and Gaul. While it is often suggested that St Patrick was the first to bring the teaching of the four gospels to these shores, it is likely that along with trade, came Christianity. Most references to St Patrick are generally found north and west of Cashel in Co. Tipperary. The coast of Co. Mayo has two places associated with St Patrick: Croagh Patrick and Downpatrick.

Croagh Patrick is easily recognised as the conical-shaped mountain rising 750m from the shores of Clew Bay, just south -west of Westport. It is known locally as 'the Reek' and from a distance a white winding path, worn by centuries of pilgrims and climbers, is clearly visible on the side of the mountain. On a fine day the sun glints off the whitewashed chapel at the summit, which was built in 1905 by locals who used donkeys to transport the necessary building materials to the site. St Patrick climbed the mountain in AD 441, where, as his Lenten penance, he spent forty days fasting and praying. Archeological finds on the summit suggest that St Patrick may not have been the first to worship there, as early Iron Age artefacts and the remains of a fifth-century church have been found. Every year, on the last Sunday in July, 25,000 pilgrims follow in the steps of St Patrick and climb Croagh Patrick, many going barefoot.

Further along the Mayo coast is the town-land of Downpatrick, where St Patrick founded a church. At this spot a large sea stack, Dún Briste (the Broken Fort), stands alone just off the shore. It is said that St Patrick was trying to convert a local chieftain to Christianity who was stubbornly resistant to St Patrick's message, preferring to hold on to his pagan ways. In frustration at his lack of success, St Patrick stuck his crozier into the ground on the cliff top with such force that a chunk of land fell away, leaving the reluctant convert stranded on the detached landmass.

The best-loved myth about St Patrick has him banishing snakes from Ireland after they attacked him while he fasted on a mountain top. If it was while he sat on top of Croagh Patrick then the last snakes in Ireland were washed into the Atlantic at Clew Bay.

WESTPORT HOUSE: THE 2ND MARQUESS OF SLIGO

Nestling in a sheltered corner of Clew Bay is one of Ireland's finest country houses. Westport House evolved over three centuries from a small fortress owned by the sixteenth-century Pirate Queen of the West, Grace O'Malley, to a fine Palladian mansion, where today part of O'Malley's castle is the dungeon. The Brownes, minor landlords in south Mayo in the seventeenth century, came into possession of this idyllic site when Colonel John Browne married Maud Bourke, a great-great granddaughter of the Pirate Queen. Colonel John Browne's grandson, also John, was the first of the family to be brought up in the Protestant faith, which opened many doors for him. He studied in Oxford, became a member of Grattan's parliament in Dublin and had ambitions for his Westport estate. In the 1730s, he engaged the German architect Richard Cassels, the most fashionable of the day and best known for building Leinster House and Russborough House, to extend and update his home. In 1771, befitting his position in Irish society, he was made an earl in the Irish peerage, becoming Lord Altamont.

The third earl, John Denis Browne, further enhanced the house by commissioning James Wyatt to decorate the interiors. In addition to working on the house, Wyatt had the village of Cahernamart, which stood in front of the house, razed to the ground. However, the Brownes were generous landlords. Not only did they provide housing for their displaced tenants, in the new town of Westport, they also developed a linen-making industry and encouraged fishing and kelp gathering. As a reward for voting in favour of the Act of Union, in 1800, John Denis was made a Marquess, becoming the Marquess of Sligo as there was already a Marquess of Mayo.

Of all the Brownes to live at Westport, Howe Peter Browne, the 2nd Marquess of Sligo, was the most colourful. He was educated at Cambridge and lived the high life in the coffee houses of London and the salons of Paris, mixing with politicians and royalty. He was friendly with the Prince Regent and Lord Byron. His interests ranged from horse racing and gambling to ballet and boxing. He once won 1,000 guineas from a bet that saw him race his coach from London to

Holyhead, a journey he made in thirty-five hours. His horse Waxy won the 1809 Epsom Derby.

That was the year that Howe Peter's father died, and aged 21 he became the 2nd Marquess, inheriting the vast estate at Westport and also sugar plantations in Jamaica. With money no object, in 1810 he set off on the usual adventure of the sons of the aristocracy: the Grand Tour. In Greece, the Marquess joined his friend, Lord Byron, who introduced him to the Governor of Morea. He had a keen interest in archaeology and hoped to secure something of antiquity to bring back to Westport. The Marquess was given access to the Treasury of Atreus, the 3,500-year-old burial place of Agamemnon, King of the Greeks. There he acquired, as souvenirs, two carved columns of green marble, which once adorned the entrance to the ancient tomb.

He had chartered a sloop, *Pylades*, for his trip to Greece and loaded the columns and other treasures on board. However, the ship's crew was work-shy and described by Byron as 'varlets'. Between the weight of the cargo and a drunken crew, by the time the Marquess reached Malta, he feared that he would not get his booty home safely. In need of more experienced crew members, he bribed two Royal Navy sailors to join *Pylades*.

The Royal Navy did not take kindly to having seamen poached during wartime and pursued *Pylades*. Once captured and returned to London, the Marquess found himself pleading his case in the Old Bailey. His mother travelled to London to plead for her son but the judge, Sir William Scott, would not be swayed and the Marquess was fined £5,000 and sentenced to four months in Newgate prison. His mother was so taken with the masterful way the judge had handled the court case that she married him, although it was not a happy marriage.

The time in prison appears to have brought a new-found maturity to Howe Peter. In 1816, he got married and went on to father fourteen children. He was a supporter of Catholic Emancipation and focused on improving the lives of his tenants on the Westport estate, where the linen industry was struggling to compete with new industrial advances in England.

In 1834 his friend, Prime Minister Robert Peel, made him Governor-General of Jamaica. The Slavery Abolition Act had been passed in London the previous year and the Marquess was tasked with implementing it in Jamaica. His arrival was hailed by the plantation owners, who assumed the new Governor, as a fellow plantation owner, would maintain the status quo. However, the relationship soon soured when they realised that the Marquess had every intention of implementing the new anti-slavery laws. He began by making changes on his own plantation, where he was disgusted at the living conditions of the slaves. Slaves were offered apprentice schemes to learn new skills, and their children were allowed schooling. By the time the Marquess left Jamaica, in 1836, part of his plantation was leased to former slaves. But there was still a long way to go before other plantation owners followed suit. On returning to London, the Marquess continued to campaign against slavery by lobbying royalty and politicians. In Jamaica, the first free slave village, Sligoville, was called after the man who Jamaicans regard as the 'Emancipator of Slaves'.

As for the plundered Grecian columns, they were abandoned in the basement of Westport House and were only discovered almost a century later, in 1904, by the son of the 5th Marquess. He retraced Peter Howe's trip to Greece, where he authenticated the columns. He then donated them to the British Museum after making replicas that still adorn an exterior door of the house today.

WESTPORT: MAJOR JOHN MACBRIDE

William Butler Yeats, in his poem 'Easter 1916', described Major John MacBride, who was executed for the part he played in the 1916 Easter Rising, as 'a drunken vainglorious lout'. Unlike Pearse, Clarke, Connolly and others, he had not called the country to arms, but he had answered that call and paid, like them, with his life. Yeats was never going to be complimentary towards MacBride, a Westport native, because he married Maud Gonne, Yeats' muse and the love of his life.

John MacBride was born into a Catholic family, at The Quay, Westport, in 1868. He was educated locally and in Belfast. By his mid teens, he was involved with the Irish Nationalist movement, taking the oath of the Irish Republican Brotherhood (IRB), an organisation dedicated to achieving Irish independence. He left Mayo and went to Dublin to study medicine, abandoning his studies to work, instead, as a pharmacist's assistant.

In 1896 the IRB sent him to America on a fundraising trip. In search of adventure, he then went to South Africa to work in a gold mine. When the second Boer War broke out in 1899 he founded and led the Irish Transvaal Brigade, fighting for the Boers against the British. MacBride saw a similarity between the Boers' plight and that of the Irish in their struggle against British rule. After the war, he could not return directly to Ireland, where he was a wanted man, so he travelled to Paris. There, his good friend Arthur Griffiths introduced him to Maud Gonne, then living in Paris. Of Anglo-Irish descent, Maud moved in Irish Nationalist and Literary Revival circles. Most notable among her friends was Yeats. Since meeting her in 1889, she had been his muse, confidant and friend. She even acted in his plays, most notably in 'Cathleen Ní Houlihan', in 1902. Yeats proposed to her several times, only to be rejected each time.

In 1903, Maud and Major MacBride were married, against the advice of almost everyone who knew them. Yeats was opposed for obvious reasons, and even MacBride's mother advised against the marriage. Their son, Sean, was born the following year, but by then the marriage was falling apart. Maud accused MacBride of drunkenness, and, controversially, of having assaulted her daughter from a previous relationship, Iseult Gonne. Over two years, their acrimonious split played out in the French courts, where a separation rather than a divorce was granted. Drunkenness was found to be MacBride's only crime. Maud won custody of Sean but MacBride was allowed visiting rights.

In 1906 MacBride returned to Dublin and never saw his son again, as Maud remained in France, although she did bring her son to visit his grandmother in Westport on one occasion.

Once back in Dublin, MacBride got a job with Dublin Corporation, collecting payments owed to the Corporation by ships using the River Liffey. He resumed his commitment to the struggle for Irish independence and, for a brief time, he was appointed to the Supreme Council of the IRB. He was replaced mainly because he was known to the British and might attract too much attention to IRB activities as they were by then planning the 1916 Easter Rising.

On that Easter Monday morning in 1916, MacBride was so out of the loop that he did not know a rebellion was happening until he encountered a group of Irish Volunteers led by Thomas MacDonagh on Grafton Street. He tagged along and marched with MacDonagh to the Jacobs Biscuit Factory, where he was appointed second-in-command because of his combat experience in South Africa. He fought bravely for a week, until the order was given to surrender.

After the Rising, the British Army decided to execute anyone who had a commanding role. While held in prison, MacBride's main concern was that he would lose his job with Dublin Corporation, little knowing the fate that awaited him. A court martial found him guilty of crimes against the Defence of the Realm Act. He was sentenced to death, and refusing a blindfold, was executed on 5 May 1916.

After his death, Maud Gonne moved back to Ireland and was known as Maud Gonne MacBride for the rest of her life, glad that her son's father had heroically died fighting for Irish independence. In 1983, a bust of John MacBride was unveiled along the canal in Westport.

Sean MacBride, John's son, became a Nobel Peace Prize winner in 1974 for his work campaigning for human rights and as a founding member of Amnesty International.

ROCKFLEET: GRACE O'MALLEY, THE PIRATE QUEEN OF THE WEST

Every coastline has a story of piracy in its past. The most notorious pirate of the Wild Atlantic Way was Grace O'Malley, a woman who lived in the sixteenth century and was known as 'Granuaile' and before the Pirate Queen of the West.

O'Malley was born into piracy around 1530. Her father, Owen Dubhdara O'Malley, made his living around Clew Bay from fishing, trading, carrying passengers and, when the opportunity arose, from piracy. By the 1530s, Ireland was a country of two distinctly different cultures. In the east, the area known as 'the Pale' was anglicised, while everywhere 'beyond the Pale' was still very much Gaelic. In Connacht, people of O'Malley's status still spoke Irish and adhered to the ancient Gaelic laws that had existed since Celtic times. All of this changed when, in 1542, King Henry VIII declared himself King of Ireland. He wanted all of Ireland to recognise him as their king, and he wanted English law to be the standard throughout Ireland. Gaelic lords were encouraged to surrender their lands, which would be restored to them along with an English title once they pledged allegiance to the King. The policy of 'Surrender and Regrant' was taken up by, among others, the Burke clan of south Galway, who were made Earls of Clanricard. Their Connemara kinsmen, however, with whom the O'Malleys were aligned, held out, leading to turmoil that would last for the rest of the century.

At the age of 16, Grace married Dónal O'Flaherty of Connemara, living for a time at Bunowen Castle, on the Galway coast. When he was killed in a skirmish with the Joyces, under Gaelic laws she was entitled to the dowry that she brought to the marriage. She returned to Clew Bay, settled on Clare Island, and with three ships and a fleet of smaller boats, she carried on her father's legacy of piracy. Her O'Flaherty connections allowed her the freedom to plunder as far south as Galway.

In 1567, Grace married Richard Burke, who owned territory around Clew Bay and Rockfleet Castle, near Newport. Grace continued her pirating escapades, basing herself at Rockfleet, which was besieged by the Sheriff of Galway in 1574. He had to retreat, as Grace and her supporters successfully defended the castle.

Richard Burke died in 1583. Throughout her life, Grace resisted the influences and laws of the English – however, she was not beyond using those laws when it suited her. By applying the English inheritance law, which granted a widow one-third of her deceased husband's estate, she came away from the marriage a much wealthier woman than under Gaelic law. With 1,000 cattle and horses, she settled at Rockfleet. However, her troubles were just beginning.

When Sir Richard Bingham was appointed Governor of Connacht in 1584, he decided that a heavy hand was the only way to get the Gaelic lords of Connacht to accept English ways. He waged war on the Burkes, and by association Grace O'Malley. By 1593 Grace had nothing. Her lands were confiscated, her ships impounded, one of her sons, Owen, dead and another, Tibbot, was a prisoner of the English. In 1593, Grace hired a boat and travelled to London, where she demanded an audience with Queen Elizabeth I.

The Pirate Queen and the Queen of England met at Greenwich Palace, where they conversed in Latin, as Grace spoke no English and Elizabeth certainly had no Irish. Grace so impressed Elizabeth that she came away with her lands restored and her son released. She was even offered the title 'Countess', which she refused, informing Elizabeth I that she was a queen in her own right. Grace promised Elizabeth that she would desist from attacking English ships. Bingham was not happy and continued to harass Grace, who returned to her pirating ways. She now had friends in high places, and he was soon removed from Connacht.

O'Malley died, possibly at Rockfleet, in 1603, the same year, coincidentally, that Elizabeth died. This legendary lady rose to fame at a time when few women made their mark in history. Since 2000, a ship bearing her name has plied its way up and down the Atlantic coast where 500 years ago she sailed. The Irish Lights vessel, which maintains 150 offshore buoys, is fittingly called *Granuaile*.

ACHILL ISLAND

In the seventeenth century, Brian Rua O'Ceabhain, a seer living in Erris, foresaw that iron carriages on wheels, breathing smoke would travel to Achill, but ominously prophesied that they would carry dead bodies.

Achill Island is the largest island on the coast of Ireland. At the end of the nineteenth century, many island dwellers lived and died without ever travelling to the mainland. The first bridge linking the Corruan Peninsula on the mainland to Achill Island was opened by and called after Michael Davitt, the Mayo-born founder of the Land League, in 1887. Previously, islanders travelling to the mainland took a ferry or, at low tide, walked. By the 1930s, the bridge, which was built in the era of horses and carts, could not cope with motorised vehicles and was replaced with a swing-bridge in 1949. The current bridge dates from 2008 and is still called the Michael Davitt bridge.

To further improve access to and from the island, the railway line from Westport was extended to Achill Sound in 1894. Passengers disembarked there and used the bridge to continue their journey on to Achill. Sadly, O'Ceabhain's prophesy came to pass when the first train to travel on the line carried the bodies of thirty-two Achill Islanders who had drowned in the Clew Bay disaster.

With no industry or jobs on the island at the end of the nineteenth century, it became traditional for the young people of Achill to leave during the summer months and seek seasonal work elsewhere. Typically they went to Scotland, between June and October, to harvest potatoes. In 1894, a group heading for Scotland left the island on a hooker (a traditional west of Ireland boat) bringing them to Westport Quay, where they were to take a steamer to Scotland. As they came close to Westport Quay, in their excitement at seeing the steamer in the bay, the passengers rushed to one side of the hooker, which capsized. The bodies of the thirty-two islanders who died were returned to the island on the new train service.

Unfortunately, that was not the end of tragedy for the migrant workers of Achill. More than forty years later, islanders were still travelling to Scotland for seasonal work. In September 1937, ten teenage youths died in a fire in their bothy-like accommodation, in Kirkintilloch, near Glasgow. They were a party of twenty-six youngsters, some brothers and sisters, who had already spent three months working on farms near Edinburgh, and were on the last job before returning home to Achill. One family lost three sons in the tragedy. Once again, the remains of the deceased were returned to their families on Achill by train. The train was making its final trip to Achill Sound as the railway line was scheduled to close. The first and last trains operating to Achill Sound fulfilled the seventeenth-century prophesy.

BLACKSOD: WEATHER READINGS DURING SECOND WORLD WAR

Under the terms of the Anglo-Irish Treaty of 1921, all 'anchorages, airfields, radio stations and undersea communications' in the newly created Irish Free State were to remain under

British control. Included in this arrangement were weather observation services. In 1936, the Irish Meteorological Service was founded and immediately set up an arrangement whereby weather readings were shared with their British counterparts. This arrangement was formalised just a few short weeks before the Second World War broke out in August 1939, and even though Ireland remained neutral, the collaboration on weather observations between the British and Irish services continued throughout the war. The main stations providing weather readings were at Malin Head, Foynes, Valencia, Roches Point and Blacksod Point.

Blacksod Point on the Mullet Peninsula is the most westerly point of Co. Mayo, where the bay offers a safe anchorage. In the village there is an Alexander Nimmo-designed pier and a lighthouse dating from 1866. It was a weather observation from Blacksod Point that led Supreme Allied Commander General Dwight D. Eisenhower to invade the Normandy beaches on 6 June 1944, the day that would be forever known as D-Day.

Operation Overlord was years in the planning. To successfully land 156,000 soldiers on the beaches of Normandy and begin the liberation of France, the Allies needed spring tides and a full moon. The dates 5, 6 and 7 June 1944 were deemed the most suitable but clear calm weather was required for the operation to be successful. The initial plan was to invade on 5 June. Group Captain James Stagg was in charge of weather forecasting for the invasion. In 1944, such forecasting was based on visual observations and readings taken by meteorologists at 500 points around the British Isles using very basic instruments. Meteorologists could only provide reliable forecasts for up to two days in advance.

Ted Sweeney was the lighthouse keeper at Blacksod Point in 1944. At 2 a.m. on the morning of 3 June, his wife, Maureen, recorded that the barometer was falling rapidly, and a force 6 wind was blowing. He relayed this information to Dublin, and the reading eventually made its way to Portsmouth and Group Captain Stagg. At 11 a.m. on 4 June, Maureen took a telephone call from a woman with an English accent, who asked if she could repeat the weather readings that had been taken earlier. The telephone rang an hour later, with the same woman looking for the latest readings. In true Irish fashion, Ted assumed that he must have made an error in the earlier readings.

However, the anonymous woman was on Group Captain Stagg's staff, and the weather reading, taken on an isolated outpost on the west coast of Ireland, was causing a stir at the headquarters of Operation Overlord. If the Blacksod weather readings were correct, it meant that the weather in the English Channel on 5 June, the day planned for the invasion of France, would be wet and windy. Stagg advised Eisenhower to delay the invasion.

The 5th dawned with low cloud and windy weather on the English Channel. Poor visibility would have impeded bomber planes, the winds would have prevented landing soldiers by parachute and the heavy seas would have made landing troops on the Normandy beaches impossible. Further weather observations predicted a break in the weather for 6 June, the day Eisenhower unleashed Operation Overlord.

Had the Allies not invaded France on D-Day, they would have had to wait for the next suitable tide and moon conditions on 19 and 20 June. The weather in the Channel on those dates in 1944 was even worse than the conditions on 5 June. The weather reading from the Sweeneys at Blacksod had changed the course of the Second World War.

THE MULLET PENINSULA:
THE CHILDREN OF LIR

One of the most popular Irish legends and known to every child in Ireland is the story of the Children of Lir. Inishglora, an island off the Mullet Peninsula, features in this popular legend, of which there are several versions. Lir was one of the Tuatha De Danan, an ancient tribe that once ruled Ireland. He lost out in a leadership race to Bodh Dearg, who, wanting to keep Lir onside, offered him one of his daughters as a wife. Lir married Eva and they had four beautiful children: a daughter Fionnula, a son Aedh and twin boys, Conn and Fiachra. When Eva died, Bodh sent another of his daughters, Aoife, to marry Lir and to look after his grandchildren. Aoife became jealous of Lir's love for his children. One day she lured them to the shores of Lough Derravargh in the midlands of Ireland. As they swam in the water, she used her magical powers to cast a spell on them, turning them into swans, but keeping their human voices. When Lir went in search of his children, he heard their voices by the lake but could only see four swans. They told him of Aoife's treachery and he reduced her to a mist, to swirl in turmoil forever. The spell on his children would only be broken after they had spent 300 years swimming Lough Derravargh, 300 years on the Sea of Moyle (between Ireland and Scotland) and 300 years on the Atlantic, near Inishglora.

For 300 years the Children of Lir swam the tranquil waters of Lough Derravargh, near their ageing father. They then flew to the Sea of Moyle, where the stormy seas threatened to separate them. After 300 years there, they flew to Inishglora. At the end of their 900 years, swimming the lakes and seas, they heard the sound of a bell on the shore of Inishglora, where St Patrick (some versions say St Brendan) baptised them and they immediately reverted to their human forms, now wizened, grey and dying. They were buried together on Inishglora.

THE CEIDE FIELDS

Along the north Mayo coastline, expansive bogland stretches inland, devoid of trees or habitation, covering acres of the land. For hundreds of years, hidden under this bog lay one of the greatest Neolithic sites in Europe and its discovery is thanks to an observant local farmer. During the 1930s, Patrick Caulfield, from Belderrig, regularly cut turf on this windswept bogland. Over the years, as he dug deeper into the bog, he found that he was uncovering piles of stones, not strewn haphazardly, as if by nature, but arranged, as if by man. If these stones were part of a manmade structure, then they were placed here centuries before the landscape was engulfed by the blanket bog. The next generation of Patrick's family continued the investigation. Using a simple method of probing the land with iron rods and marking the arrangement of stones, it was found that lines of stones ran parallel to each other, inland from the coast. At intervals these walls were intersected with other walls, connecting the parallels. The Cauldfields had discovered the oldest known field system in the world, buried under the bog at Ceide.

Further archaeological investigations have since revealed that the Ceide Fields date from between 3700 BC and 3200 BC, during the Neolithic period. When Stone Age man first arrived at Ceide, it was covered in oak and birch forest. The trees were cleared and used for fuel and tools, and the cleared land was cultivated for farming. Stones, strewn across the land, were gathered and used to build dry stone walls. The uncut stones were built up by fitting and balancing them together, with no mortar used to secure them. The dry stone walls at the Ceide Fields were probably the first built in Ireland. The same method has been used ever since to build walls that are a feature of rural Ireland to this day.

With the land divided into manageable plots, the Neolithic people ploughed the fields and planted wheat and barley. Parts of an ancient wooden plough were discovered at the site. Cattle were also farmed and there is evidence that the farmers used manure to fertilise the soil. A field system such as this would not be seen in the British Isles again until the eighteenth century.

Also at Ceide, there is evidence of circular dwelling places. Pieces of pottery from the Neolithic period have also been discovered. The presence of portal and court tombs, close to the field system, suggests that the community was settled and not nomadic. While archaeological research at the Ceide Fields has provided valuable information about the Neolithic period in Ireland, archaeology cannot tell how these Neolithic people organised their settlement.

Climate change may have played a part in the demise of the settlement. As the climate grew colder, the growing year contracted. Also, after centuries of farming the same land intensively, the yield from crops would have decreased as nutrients were leached from the soil. From 2700 BC, the farmland was abandoned. Rainfall and lack of shelter from trees contributed to the spread of blanket bogs, which engulfed the abandoned farmland. The dry stone walls were hidden under the boggy depths until they were rediscovered in the twentieth century when the turf was stripped away for fuel, once again revealing the labours of our dry stone wall-building ancestors.

7

COUNTY SLIGO AND COUNTY LEITRIM

KNOCKNAREA: QUEEN MAEVE'S GRAVE

Knocknarea, 'the Hill of Kings', is a lone hill south of Sligo that was once the site where Kings of Connacht were crowned. The visible mound on top of the hill is a yet-to-be excavated passage tomb. Although this is the Hill of Kings, the mound is known locally as Queen Maeve's Grave. Her story is based in Celtic mythology and is one of murder, jealousy, theft and war. This legendary Queen of Connacht, if she existed, lived around AD 50 and, as with all legend, her story has been embellished as it passed down through the ages.

Her father was King of Connacht, then rose to become High King of Ireland. He arranged Maeve's marriage to the King of Ulster, Concobhar Mac Nessa, the first of Maeve's five husbands. They had a son but after a year of marriage Concobhar had enough of the troublesome Maeve and sent her back to her father. To keep the peace, her father sent his younger daughter, Eithne, to Ulster as a replacement. At some point in her story, in a fit of jealousy, Maeve murdered Eithne, whose son Furbaid then vowed revenge. Recognising that Maeve had a mind of her own, the High King made Maeve Queen of Connacht, where her continued troublemaking eventually led to war.

One day Queen Maeve and Aillil Mac Máta, another of her husbands, were arguing over which of them had the most wealth. After comparing their gold, jewels, and even their livestock, Maeve was relieved that they were equally wealthy. Then Aillil produced the White Bull he owned, of which Maeve had no equal. Annoyed that she, the Queen of Connacht, should not be as wealthy as her husband, Maeve sent messengers the length and breadth of Ireland to find the most valuable bull, with orders to steal it if necessary.

They found the Brown Bull of Cooley in Ulster, the finest specimen of a bull in Ireland, but the owner was not willing to sell. Queen Maeve was so determined to have the Brown Bull that she declared war on her first husband, Concobhar. Unfortunately his army, the Red Branch Knights, were under a spell cast by Macha, a fairy who died at the hands of Concobhar. The spell saw them all fall ill before a critical battle. Only Cuchulainn was immune to the spell, so Concobhar sent him to defend Ulster single-handedly. He died in the fight, which is another story, and the Brown Bull of Cooley was brought to Connacht. Not content with owning the most prized bull in Ireland, Maeve then killed Aillil, so that she could own the White Bull, too. However, when the bulls were put in the same field together, the Brown Bull of Cooley killed the White Bull, scattering his body all over Connacht. He escaped and rambled back to Ulster. In the meantime, the Red Branch Knights released from the spell, invaded Connacht and defeated Queen Maeve's army.

Maeve's past eventually caught up with her when her vengeful nephew Furbaid tracked her down. One day, he came upon Maeve while she was bathing in a Sligo river. He hit her with a piece of hard cheese fired from a slingshot, killing her. This legendary Queen of Connacht was buried on the top of

Knocknarea in a standing pose, dressed in her armour and facing north in the direction of Ulster.

CARROWMORE: IRELAND'S LARGEST ANCIENT BURIAL GROUND

One of the most significant prehistoric sites along the Wild Atlantic Way is the extensive megalithic burial ground at Carrowmore, on the Coolrea Peninsula, south of Sligo and in the shadow of Knocknarea. Covering an area of 60 hectares, this cemetery boasts the largest collection of portal tombs in Ireland. Unfortunately, the first people to explore the site at Carrowmore were eighteenth-century treasure hunters rather than true archaeologists. They carried off ancient artefacts that were either sold or displayed in their own collections. In the process they disturbed clues that could have explained the monuments' history.

Thankfully, by the nineteenth century, more enlightened people came to survey Carrowmore. Roger Walker, of Rathcarrick House, owned the land at Carrowmore. He was friendly with George Petrie, who worked for the Ordnance Survey Office. In 1837, at Walker's invitation, Petrie, who is regarded as the father of archaeology in Ireland, visited Carrowmore. He began meticulously mapping the site and, unlike his predecessors, took a scientific approach to his work by assigning a unique number to each of the tombs, drawing each as it appeared at that time, and producing a large site map. To this day, archaeologists working on Carrowmore still use the numbers that Petrie assigned to each tomb. Since the 1830s, archaeologists have continued to survey Carrowmore, using modern techniques and equipment, giving us the kind of insights of which Petrie could only have dreamed. Petrie's

research in the 1830s identified sixty-five tombs on the site, and there may have been more. Modern archaeologists have identified just thirty portal tombs at Carrowmore. Over the centuries, farming, quarrying and even nature itself have all intervened to alter the site.

A portal tomb, or dolmen, is made up of three to six megaliths, upon which a large capstone is placed, often slightly tilted, making them look like giant stone tables. The remains of the dead were buried in the sheltered area between the stones. The Carrowmore tombs are thought to date from between 4000 and 3000 BC. The most important tomb at Carrowmore is No. 51, as labelled by Petrie, and is named Listoghil.

Listoghil is made up of a large limestone slab laid on top of six megaliths. This enormous stone only touches two of the upright stones, and sits at a 6 degree tilt off the horizontal. The architects of this structure used sandstone wedges to secure it to the other stones. It differs from the other tombs in several ways. To begin with, there are decorative carvings on the side of the capstone. Secondly, while the human remains found at all of the other tombs were cremated, human bones were found in and near Listoghil. Analysis of these bones suggests that seven people were buried here, and one bone fragment came from a male in his fifties, a great age for someone living in the Stone Age. Thirdly, Listoghil is aligned with the sunrise on 31 October, the old Celtic feast of Samhain, and modern-day Halloween, although the tomb pre-dates any Celtic festivals. Finally, and quite significantly, Listoghil was, at one time, covered by a cairn. Like at Newgrange in the Boyne Valley, where the passage tomb is covered by a mound of stones, the dolmen of Listoghil was also covered. While archaeologists think this cairn was added at a later date than the original construction of the dolmen, they are unsure if there was a passage leading to the dolmen under the cairn.

Today the Office of Public Works looks after the Carrowmore site and some of the work carried out in recent years has been controversial. Listoghil has been partially surrounded by a stone structure in an effort to recreate the cairn that once covered it. This structure is, at least, better than what was planned for Carrowmore in the 1980s, when Sligo County Council proposed using part of the site as a refuse tip. In 1983, local and historical interest groups challenged the local authority's plan in the High Court. That court, unbelievably, decided that Sligo County Council should be allowed to go ahead with the planned refuse tip, under certain conditions. The case was appealed to the Supreme Court, where the High Court decision was overruled.

And what of the archaeological treasures taken from the site in the early 1800s? Most of these items, which included pottery vessels, flint weapons, pins, pendants and a twisted gold torc, remained in Roger Walker's collection of antiquities. However, a year before he died, he sold all of these pieces to the 4th Duke of Northumberland for £300. They were displayed in the museum at Alnwick Castle until they were bought at a Sotheby's auction by the National Museum of Ireland in 1990.

SLIGO: THE DOMINICAN FRIARY

In the ninth century, the invading Vikings built the first Irish
towns. Dublin, Waterford and Limerick all owe their origins
to the fiery invaders and all were thriving urban settlements
long before the first town was built in the north-west. In
1243, the Anglo-Norman Maurice Fitzgerald built a castle
at 'Sligeach', the 'shelly place', where the shallow Garavogue
river flows into Sligo Bay. In due course, the town of Sligo built
up around the castle. With a foothold in north Connacht, the
Anglo-Normans could continue their conquest northward,
towards Ulster. Ten years later, Fitzgerald had a Dominican
Friary built in the town, and while the castle is long gone,
the ruins of Sligo Abbey remain and are some of the most
impressive monastic ruins along the Wild Atlantic Way.

The Dominicans were dedicated to preaching the teachings
of Jesus Christ and saving souls. Unlike other orders who
remained in the confines of the abbey, the Dominican friars
went out into the community to preach. They also allowed
the faithful to worship at the friary church.

An unattended candle caused a fire in the original friary
in 1414 and funding to rebuild it came from indulgences,
offered by the Pope, to anyone who donated to the restoration.
Most of what remains of Sligo Abbey today dates from the
fifteenth century.

Among the interesting features is a Rood Screen ('rood'
is a Saxon word for 'cross'), which was used to separate the
congregation from the friars and the church altar. In the medieval
period, the laity were not deemed worthy enough to witness the
solemn consecration of the Catholic mass. Also of note is the
stone high altar, which is one of the only remaining examples in
Ireland. Nine carved, cusped arches decorate the front.

As with any medieval church, the tombs are noteworthy. In the nave, the most decorative is the O'Crean tomb, which dates from 1506. The chest tomb is adorned with nine arched niches, similar to those on the high altar. Each niche has a carved figure, with St Dominic, St Catherine, the Blessed Virgin Mary, and possibly St Patrick just some of the religious figures represented. An elaborately carved canopy hangs over the tomb.

On the south wall, overlooking the altar, is a memorial to Sir Donagh O'Connor, Lord Sligo, and his wife, Elinor Butler, dating from 1624. The couple are depicted at the centre, kneeling and facing each other, surrounded by symbols of life and the after-life, and topped by their coats of arms under a crucifix. Sir Donagh was instrumental in persuading Queen Elizabeth I not to dissolve the friary, as was the fate of most monasteries during the Tudor era.

The abbey was attacked and badly damaged in July 1642.

Sir Frederick Hamilton's castle at Manorhamilton was attacked by the Gaelic O'Rourkes and in retaliation he ruthlessly burnt Sligo to the ground, killing almost 300 people. He then turned his ire on the friars at the abbey, some of whom were murdered while fleeing their burning church. The Dominicans later returned to Sligo Abbey and remained there until the 1760s. After the friars left the abbey, the building crumbled; however, some restoration work was carried out in the nineteenth century. Wilfred Ashley was the last private owner before he gifted the abbey to the Board of Works in 1913.

SLIGO: THE POLLEXFEN FAMILY

Co. Sligo is known as Yeats Country, after the poet William Butler Yeats, and yet he never lived permanently in the county. His mother, Susan Pollexfen, however, was a native of Sligo. Her family were prominent merchants there during the nineteenth century.

Elizabeth Pollexfen was the first of the family to come to the town. She came, as a 15-year-old bride, in 1813, from her home on Jersey. There she had met her husband, William Middleton, a sea captain and smuggler. They settled in Sligo, where Middleton set up respectable shipping and milling businesses. A cholera outbreak in 1832 killed William, leaving Elizabeth widowed with two young children and businesses to run. Her second cousin, William Pollexfen, from Cornwall, sailed into Sligo on board his merchant ship *The Dasher* and offered to help her run her late husband's businesses. He eventually married Elizabeth's daughter, also Elizabeth, and ran the family business with Elizabeth's son, William Jr. By the 1850s, the Middleton–Pollexfens were a thriving Sligo merchant family. In 1857, they established the Sligo Steam Navigation Company, the first to operate steam ships out of Sligo. By the 1860s, the company owned twenty-five ships, was carrying cargo as far as the Black Sea and operated passenger services to Belfast, Glasgow, Liverpool, and across the Atlantic.

With business flourishing, they built new offices and warehouses on Wine Street. A feature of that building, today the Pollexfen Building, is a turret protruding from the roof. In the heyday of the Sligo Steam Navigation Co., William Pollexfen would climb to the turret, telescope at the ready, and look over the rooftops of Sligo towards the port and watch as his ships came and went. On the death of William Middleton Jr in 1882 the fortunes of the company began to wane.

William and Elizabeth's daughter, Susan, married John Butler Yeats in 1863, a friend of her brother's. In 1865, their son, William Butler Yeats, was born in Dublin. He would spend many of his childhood summers in Sligo, staying with the Pollexfens.

RATHCORMACK: COUNTESS MARKIEVICZ

At the village of Rathcormack, on a sweeping bend in the road, stands a statue of a woman in revolutionary pose. The simple inscription reads 'Markievicz', not the most Irish of names. Fittingly, this statue of Countess Markievicz, unveiled on Easter Monday in 2003 and created by the sculptor John Coll, is facing towards Lissadell House, her ancestral family home about 10km away.

Constance Gore Booth was born in London in 1868, daughter of Henry and Georgina Gore Booth, an established family of the Sligo gentry. Like most girls of her position and generation, Constance was educated at home by a governess. Her father allowed her to study at the Slade School of Art in London. This interest in art took her to Paris, where she met Count Casimir Markievicz, an aristocratic Polish artist. Constance and Casimir were married in London in 1900, and a year later their daughter, Maeve, was born at Lissadell.

While Constance and Casimir mixed with a Bohemian set in Dublin, which included people such as Maud Gonne and William Butler Yeats, her younger sister, Eva, left Lissadell and moved to Manchester. There, she began campaigning for better conditions for the poor, for women and, most particularly, for Irish immigrants. Constance soon joined Eva in her political activities and in 1908 they foiled an election bid by Winston Churchill.

Parliament was concerned about the excessive consumption of alcohol by the working classes. One politician suggested that by employing men rather than barmaids the public houses would be less attractive places for men to visit. Eva founded the Barmaids Political Defence League to support the soon-to-be-unemployed barmaids. A by-election was held in Manchester that year in which Winston Churchill was the Liberal candidate. His Conservative opponent, William Joyson-Hicks, did not stand a chance. However, like the Gore Booth sisters, Joyson-Hicks was against banning barmaids from the alehouses. The Sligo sisters campaigned vigorously for him and he won the seat, much to the shock of the British political establishment. (Churchill won a parliamentary seat in another by-election later that year.) When, in later months, the Barmaid Bill was put before the House of Commons, it was defeated and the barmaids kept their jobs.

Soon Constance was taking an interest in Irish politics and despite coming from an Anglo-Irish family, believed that Ireland should have independence from British rule. At Maud Gonne's encouragement, she joined Inghinidhe na hEireann (Daughters of Ireland), a political, social and cultural organisation promoting Irish independence, women's suffrage and the Irish language. The writings of Arthur Griffiths, founder of Sinn Féin, prompted her to join his political party in 1908, and then she joined the Irish Citizen Army, which was set up by the Dublin trade union movement to protect workers during the 1913 Lockout. Inevitably, when the time came for rebellion, she played an active part. On that Easter Monday in

1916 when the Rising against British rule broke out in Dublin she helped commandeer the Royal College of Surgeons on St Stephen's Green, where she was second-in-command. On surrendering the building at the end of Easter week, the British officer in charge of the arrests offered Countess Markievicz a lift to the barracks in an army vehicle. She refused, saying she would march with her men, behind the vehicle.

Those who had command roles during the Easter Rising were sentenced to death and this included the Countess. Eva came to Dublin to plead for her sister's life; however, Constance had declared that she was ready to die for Ireland. This was not to be. As a suffragette, she was disappointed when her sentence was commuted to penal servitude for life because of her gender. She was sent to Aylesbury Prison in England, and was released under a 1917 amnesty granted to those who had fought in the Rising. However, in 1918 the Countess and other prominent Sinn Féiners were rearrested, as the British feared that they could be planning another rebellion. This new wave of arrests only strengthened the resolve of Irish Nationalists, and also rallied the support of the Irish public.

The end of the First World War in December 1918 led to a General Election in Great Britain and Ireland. Sinn Féin fielded candidates in every Irish constituency, promising their electorate that if elected, their members would not take their seats in Westminster, but would form their own independent parliament in Dublin. Seventy-three Sinn Féin candidates were elected, including Countess Markievicz, who became the Member of Parliament for St Patrick's South Dublin constituency. Of the eighteen female candidates who ran in the 1918 General Election, Countess Markievicz was the only one elected. She, therefore, became the first women ever elected to the House of Commons in Westminster. However, in keeping with Sinn Féin's policy of abstention, she never took her seat in London. Instead, on 21 January 1919, in the Round Room of the Mansion House, Dublin, she took her seat in the first Irish parliament or Dáil Eireann. Countess Markievicz was appointed Minister of Labour and, in another first, she became the first woman in Europe to be granted a ministerial role.

After the Treaty negotiations of 1921, which led to the founding of the Irish Free State and partitioned Ireland, the Countess sided with Éamon de Valera in his opposition to the Treaty. She joined his Fianna Fáil Party when it was founded in 1926 and was elected to the Dáil again in 1927. She became ill shortly afterwards and died at Sir Patrick Dun's Hospital from appendicitis. Thousands lined the streets as this revolutionary woman was brought for burial to Dublin's Glasnevin Cemetery, where de Valera read a graveside oration.

The statue at Rathcormac reminds travellers of this aristocratic lady who championed the poor and fought against her own class in the struggle for Irish independence.

DRUMCLIFFE: YEATS' GRAVE

Much has been written about the poems, plays and politics of the great Irish poet William Butler Yeats. Although not born in Sligo, he regarded it as his spiritual home. Such was his affection for the county that he wrote in the poem *Under Ben Bulben* that he wished to be buried under the majestic sweep of Ben Bulben, in the churchyard of Drumcliffe, where an ancestor was once a rector. The ancestor in question was his paternal great-grandfather, who served as rector for the parish of Drumcliffe in the early 1800s.

St Colmcille founded a sixth-century monastery at Drumcliffe. The stump of what was once a round tower, the only round tower in Co. Sligo, and an eleventh-century Celtic High Cross are all that remains of Drumcliffe's early Christian past. In a simple grave, outside the door of the Anglican Church, which was built in the 1840s, and with Ben Bulben as a backdrop, is Yeats's grave.

Yeats spent many of his childhood summers with his maternal grandparents in Sligo and the folklore, myth and legend of the region inspired his earlier poetry. In 1899 he co-founded the Irish Literary Theatre, which later became the Abbey Theatre, and he became a senator in the new Irish Free State on its foundation in 1921. He won a Nobel Prize for literature in 1923. He was a husband to George Hyde Lees, and a father to two children, Michael and Anne.

In his later years he moved with his wife to the south of France in the hope that the warmer climate would improve his health. The couple stayed at the Hotel Idéal Séjour in the village of Menton, on the French Riviera. George was aware that, on his death, Yeats wished to be buried in Sligo. However, he told her that if he died in France, he was to be buried there for a year and when the fuss had died down and the press had lost interest, he said, 'Plant me in Sligo.' He died on 28 January 1939 in Roquebrune-Cap Martin. As per his wishes, George bought a grave in the local churchyard, overlooking the Mediterranean Sea, and there she buried her husband.

The family had fully intended bringing Yeats' remains back to Ireland within a year of his death, however, the Second World War intervened and arrangements to repatriate Yeats were not made until 1948. The Irish state assisted the Yeats family in the repatriation of Ireland's most famous poet. An Irish naval vessel, LE *Macha*, was sent to Nice to bring Yeats home. As Sligo docks could not accommodate a ship of that size, LE *Macha* docked in Galway, on 17 September 1948. Family members went on board before Yeats was brought, once more, on to Irish soil. The cortège travelled by road to Sligo and on to Drumcliffe, where, on a wet Sligo day at a simple graveside service attended by crowds of people, he was laid to rest, as per his original wishes.

However, all was not as it seemed. In France, as grave space is limited, it is traditional for graves to be cleared after a few years and relics removed to a communal ossuary tomb. Yeats' grave had been bought for ten years even though it was intended to repatriate him to Ireland the following year. Unfortunately, in 1946, Yeats' French grave was cleared and his remains were put in the ossuary. Documents belonging to a French diplomat who dealt with the repatriation were discovered as recently as 2015 in a French chateau. They confirmed that French officials knew that Yeats' remains were in the communal ossuary. They assembled a collection of bones to be sent to Ireland, but could not be certain that they all belonged to Yeats.

Whether all or part of William Butler Yeats is buried at Drumcliffe makes no difference. His memory is kept alive by the 180,000 visitors to his graveside each year, many of whom no doubt try to interpret his self-penned epitaph: 'Cast a cold eye, on life on death, horseman pass by.'

STREEDAGH BEACH: THE SPANISH ARMADA

Along the length of the Wild Atlantic Way there are many sites where ships from King Philip II's Spanish Armada foundered. At low tide, the remains of three wrecked Armada ships are visible on Streedagh Beach. Under the water, buried in the shifting sands, are possessions and artefacts lost on a fateful day in September 1588.

In May 1588, King Philip II dispatched a fleet of 130 ships carrying 30,000 soldiers to invade England. He planned to overthrow the Protestant Queen Elizabeth I and restore Catholicism. Under the command of the Duke of Medina Sidonia, on the flagship San Martin, the Spanish Armada engaged with the English Navy at the Battle of Gravelines, in the English Channel, at the end of July. After two weeks of battle, King Philip's plan was in tatters. Six of his galleons were lost during the battle, and the surviving ships, badly battered and broken, began drifting, not south and homewards, but northwards, up the eastern side of England. Their only hope of returning to Spain was to travel around Scotland and down the west coast of Ireland. With no accurate charts for the area, ships sailed south, keeping the land in view on the port side, on the assumption that the west coast of Ireland was a straight line, from Donegal to Kerry. The protruding landmass of Co. Mayo and Connemara caught some ships unawares. To add to their woes, they were further hampered by storms and headwinds.

The Lord Deputy of Ireland, William Fitzwilliam, ordered that all Spanish ships sailing along the coast of Ireland were to be seized, their stores and treasures confiscated and all on board were to be executed. He also ordered that anyone found assisting the Spanish would be executed. This was directed at the Catholic Gaelic lords of the north-west, who were sympathetic to the Spanish mission. Many ignored the threat, one notable example being the MacSweeneys of Donegal, who helped fix the broken rudder of *Girona* at Killybegs.

Further south, the Spaniards did not meet with such kindness. In Co. Clare, Sheriff Boetius Clancy followed Fitzwilliam's instruction to the letter, executing sixty Spaniards who had survived the wrecking of the *San Marcos* and *San Esteban* off the Clare coast. The nearby village became known as Spanish Point. The O'Flaherys of Connemara captured 300 Spanish prisoners and handed them over to Sir Richard Bingham, Governor of Connacht, who had them all executed. When the executioners had finished their grisly task, the people of Galway buried the dead and found two Spaniards who were still alive. They were spirited out of the city to the Aran Islands, from where they eventually made it back to Spain.

It is estimated that twenty-six ships foundered on the west coast of Ireland, with the loss of 9,000 lives, during September 1588. By late October, the threat was over. English fears that the Spaniards would gain a foothold in Ireland and drum up Catholic support among the Gaelic lords had abated. Bingham reported to Dublin that only a few 'begging sick men' were all that remained of the Spanish presence in Ireland.

One of those 'beggars' was Captain Francisco De Cuéllar who, amid all the horror and carnage, had a remarkable story of survival. De Cuéllar was an experienced seafarer who captained the *San Pedro* at Gravelines but he fell foul of his superiors for disobeying orders during the battle. At a court martial, De Cuéllar denied the charge, but was found guilty and sentenced to death. Stripped of his captaincy, he was put on board *Lavia*, which like most of the fleeing ships, was travelling northwards towards Scotland, his execution put on hold until the ship reached Spain.

By late September, *Lavia*, along with *Santa Maria de Visón* and *La Juliana*, carrying 1,100 soldiers and sailors, was travelling south past the Sligo coast. A storm forced the ships to take shelter in Sligo Bay. For three days, they anchored there, praying for the winds to change and carry them back out to sea. On 25 September 1588, a fresh storm brought a wind change, but not in the direction they wanted. The gales were of such force that the ships broke anchor and were blown on to Streedagh Beach. Already severely damaged, the ships broke up and sank. Hundreds of sailors trapped on board were drowned. Those who managed to jump overboard perished in the tossing seas. For the 300 Spaniards who reached the shore, a worse fate awaited them. English soldiers and local Irish, loyal to the Crown, who had been watching and waiting, were lined along the beach. Spanish noblemen, high-ranking naval officers and ordinary soldiers were cut down and their bodies stripped of all of their possessions.

De Cuéllar, who could not swim, jumped overboard from the *Lavia*, injuring his leg in the process. He used a hatch cover to keep afloat and managed to drift to the shore. There, battered and blood-soaked, he made his way, undetected, to the sand dunes, where he hid. This was the beginning of a seven-month struggle in Ireland. He recounts all that happened to him in a letter that he wrote on reaching the safety of Spanish Flanders in October 1589.

He encountered the worst and the best of the Irish in the seven months he spent trying to flee Ireland. He first sought refuge at Staad Abbey, only to find twelve of his compatriots hanging from the rafters. He was robbed of all his possessions by opportunists, but was later given hospitality by Brian O'Rourke of Breffine and the McClancys of Rossclough. He met other Spaniards along the way, joining one group who were making their way to Killybegs. They had heard *Girona* was anchored there waiting for escapees. However, De Cuéllar's injured leg prevented him from keeping up with his friends and he missed the sailing. *Girona* sank near the Giant's Causeway with the loss of all but nine of those on board. Having had a lucky escape, with help from the Catholic Bishop of Derry he eventually left Ireland on a very flimsy boat, heading for the Shetland Islands. By October 1589 he had reached Spanish Flanders and safety. Francisco De Cuéllar's death sentence was commuted, he returned to sea and the last known record of him is in New Spain (Mexico) in 1606.

CLASSIEBAWN

Skirting Donegal Bay, approaching the village of Mullaghmore, the eye cannot but be drawn to the house of towers and turrets perched on a hill overlooking the harbour. With no trees surrounding it, Classiebawn Castle stands tall, against the harsh Atlantic weather. Images of this wind-swept house and Mullaghmore were pitched on to the front pages of the world's newspapers when, on 27 August 1979, Lord Louis Mountbatten, uncle of the late Duke of Edinburgh, was murdered by the IRA in the harbour.

Ownership of the castle came to Lord Mountbatten through marriage. Until the seventeenth century, this stretch of the Atlantic coast was ruled by the O'Connors, Gaelic lords who refused to be anglicised. Cromwell caught up with them in the 1650s, confiscated their lands and granted 4,000 hectares to Sir John Temple, then Master of the Rolls in Ireland. Sir John never once set foot on his Co. Sligo lands but he and his descendants reaped the financial rewards. Temple's Victorian descendant, Henry, 3rd Viscount Palmerston, Foreign Secretary and later

Prime Minister of Great Britain and Ireland, did visit his estate. During the summer months, he stayed regularly at Cliffony and began making plans to build a more permanent summer house at the village of Mullaghmore. He contracted Dublin architect J. Rawson Carrol, who also designed Sligo Courthouse, to build a Victorian baronial manor house. Palmerston also paid to have a harbour and a row of cottages for local fishermen built in the village.

Sadly, Henry died in 1874 before Classiebawn Castle was completed. His stepson, William Cowper Temple, inherited the estate and, as he had no children, the property passed to his nephew, the Honorable Evelyn Ashley, 2nd Lord Temple and grandfather of Edwina Ashley. She and Lord Mountbatten were married in 1922. As a child, Edwina had visited Classiebawn regularly for fishing and shooting holidays. When Ireland erupted in rebellion in 1916, her family moved everything out of Classiebawn and shuttered the house. For a period during the Civil War in 1922 it was reopened to accommodate soldiers of the Free State Army.

When her father died in 1939, she inherited Classiebawn but during the Second World War the Mountbattens had no time to visit their decaying Irish inheritance. Throughout the war, Lord Mountbatten served as Admiral of the Fleet of the Royal Navy, while Edwina worked tirelessly for St John's Ambulance. They were in India until 1947, where Lord Mountbatten was the last Viceroy before India gained independence.

In the early 1950s Classiebawn was modernised with electricity and refurbished to accommodate the Mountbatten family who, until 1979, spent their family summers there. Even after Edwina died in 1960, Lord Mountbatten continued to visit. When the Northern Ireland troubles escalated in the 1970s Lord Mountbatten knew that he was a possible target for an IRA attack because of his relationship with British Royalty. He was advised not to make his usual summer visits but, undeterred, he continued to holiday at Classiebawn, even refusing extra security.

In 1979, the family came to Mullaghmore as usual. After a summer of wet weather, the morning of 27 August dawned brighter than it had been for days. Lord Mountbatten decided to take his boat out into the bay to check lobster pots. *Shadow V* was kept at Mullaghmore harbour and it was common knowledge that the boat belonged to the Mountbattens.

On the boat with Lord Mountbatten that morning was Paul Maxwell, a 15-year-old from Enniskillen, whose family regularly spent part of the summer in Mullaghmore. That year, he was given the job of maintaining the boat. Also in the party was Pamela Knatchbull, Lord Mountbatten's daughter, her husband John, John's mother Lady Doreen Brabourne and finally Nicholas and Timothy Knatchbull, the 14-year-old twin sons of Pamela and John.

They were not long out to sea when those onshore heard a massive bang. It did not take the locals and those in boats on the bay long to realise what had happened. *Shadow V* had exploded. Lord Mountbatten, Paul Maxwell and Nicholas Knatchbull were killed instantly. Lady Brabourne died later in hospital and the survivors, Pamela, John and Timothy Knatchbull, all spent time in Sligo General Hospital being treated for horrific wounds.

The IRA was responsible for the murders. That same day they killed eighteen British soldiers in an ambush at Warrenpoint, making 27 August 1979 one of the worst days of the Northern Ireland Troubles. The culprits were found quickly and charged with the murder of Lord Mountbatten, Lady Brabourne and the two teenagers. The family left Classiebawn and never spent another summer there again. Prince Charles, who was very close to Lord Mountbatten, who he knew as 'Uncle Dickie', made a poignant visit to Mullaghmore in 2015.

THE ANNALS OF THE FOUR MASTERS

The religious policies of sixteenth-century Tudor monarchs led to the closure of most monasteries throughout the British Isles. The Irish Franciscans went to Leuven (Louvain in French), in Spanish Flanders, where in 1607 the Papacy granted them the privilege to open an Irish College to educate Irish priests. One Irish cleric who attended the college was Tadgh Ó'Cléirigh. Born near Creevy in Donegal in about 1590, he came from a family of renowned poets and scholars. He joined the Franciscan Order, where he took the religious name Brother Mícheál, never taking Holy Orders. In Leuven, he was soon immersed in the study of manuscripts. His mentor, Hugh Ward, sent him back to Ireland in 1627, tasked with writing an annal of the Saints of Ireland. In search of information, Brother Mícheál visited monasteries and castles, reading and transcribing manuscripts and annals. In these documents, he found both religious and secular histories. On 22 January 1632, Brother Mícheál and three fellow scribes embarked on a broader, more secular, project: to write a complete history of Ireland. It was originally titled, *Annála Rioghachta na hEireann, The Annals of the Kingdom of Ireland*, but it became known as *The Annals of the Four Masters*.

Having secured patronage from the wealthiest of Sligo's Gaelic Lords, Fearghal O'Gara, the four historians worked at the Franciscan community, displaced from Donegal town, and now living in humble quarters on the Leitrim side of the Drowes river, near where it flows into Donegal Bay. Brother

Mícheál's fellow scribes were all lay members of the Franciscan Order. Cú Coigcríghe Ó'Cléirigh, his distant cousin, had started working on a history of Irish saints in 1624 and some of this work was transcribed into *The Annals of the Four Masters*. Cú Coigcríche Uí Diubhgeannaín, better known by his religious name Peregrine, was from Leitrim, and the fourth 'master' was Fearfease Uí Maolchonaire from Roscommon. For a month, during the four years it took to write the Annals, Conaire Ó'Cléirigh, Brother Mícheál's brother, also made a contribution. They gathered the information needed from ancient manuscripts, many written on vellum, such as *The Annals of Clonmacnoise*, *The Annals of Ulster*, *The Annals of the Island of Saints* and *The Annals of Kilronan*, among others. From these, the friars compiled lists of the genealogy of Gaelic clans, the successions of the High Kings, battles and wars, bards and saints, disasters and disease.

The Annals of the Four Masters starts at the year 2242 BC, after the Creation, and forty days before the Great Flood for which Noah built the Ark. In the absence of documentation from this period, the masters relied on myth and legend for the earliest entries. The first entry relates to the arrival of a woman called Ceasair, who, with her followers, were the first people to settle in Ireland. An entry for AD 432 announces the arrival of St Patrick. A later entry, dated 1472, recounts the first appearance of a camel in Ireland, sent by the King of England, Edward IV. The final entry of *The Annals of the Four Masters* is dated 1616 and records the death, in Rome, of Hugh O'Neill, Earl of Tyrone. As all hope of preserving Gaelic Ireland from the spread of English rule died with him, the end of an era was a fitting final entry.

The four scribes finished their work on 10 August 1636. Of the two copies they made, one was given to their benefactor,

Fearghal O'Gara, and Brother Mícheál brought the other to the Irish College in Leuven, where it was to be printed. This never came to pass.

Brother Mícheál saw his work as vital to preserving the story of Ireland for future generations. He predicted that the old manuscripts that he had used as sources of information would decay or be lost in centuries to come, little knowing that, within a decade, Oliver Cromwell and his soldiers would begin that destruction.

What has become of these manuscripts? The Leuven book was moved to Rome during religious upheaval on the Continent, while the O'Gara copy came into the possession of a branch of the O'Connor clan, but was then, controversially, given to the library of the Duke of Buckingham in the eighteenth century. Today, all the manuscripts are in Dublin, where volumes of the Leuven book are held by University College Dublin and the Royal Irish Academy (RIA) and volumes of the O'Gara book are held by the RIA and Trinity College.

While there have been some translations of the work, the best-regarded is the work of the eminent Irish scholar John O'Donovan who, between 1848 and 1851, translated *The Annals of the Four Masters* into English, providing helpful footnotes that have been invaluable to scholars of Irish history.

Ireland owes a debt of gratitude to these four scholars. The greatest debt is owed to Brother Mícheál Ó'Cléirigh, who walked Ireland in search of the necessary manuscripts to fulfil his life's ambition of compiling the first comprehensive history of Ireland.

8

COUNTY DONEGAL

ROSSNOWLAGH

On the Saturday preceding 12 July each year, an unusual event takes place at the quiet seaside village of Rossnowlagh. Up to 10,000 people converge on the village and the sound of pipe and drum bands fills the air, as the only annual Orange Order Parade that takes place in the Republic of Ireland files its way from St John's Church to the wide beach. The marching season is a tradition more associated with Northern Ireland, where Orange Lodges, affiliated to the Presbyterian church, commemorate the victory of King William III of Orange over his Catholic father-in-law, King James II, at the Battle of the Boyne on 12 July 1690.

The Orange Order was founded in 1796 to promote Protestantism in Ireland and loyalty to the Crown. The brethren of the Order, north of the Border, march on 12 July each year, wearing orange sashes and bowler hats. On the foundation of the Irish Free State, Orange Order marches continued to take place in the Ulster counties of Donegal, Monaghan and Cavan, which were not included in Northern Ireland. In the early 1930s, however, following threats of violence from certain Republican quarters, these ceased and Orange Lodges based in the counties south of the border marched, instead, at parades throughout Northern Ireland.

That is until the late 1930s, when a small parade took place at the quiet, secluded seaside village of Rossnowlagh. The numbers attending were modestly in the hundreds but in 1969, as the Northern Ireland troubles escalated, it was decided to cancel the parade planned for July 1970, as there was concern that it could be a flashpoint for conflict. It was revived again in 1978. Ever since then, the parade has grown in popularity and by 1993 the crowd was estimated at 10,000. Today a gathering of up to fifty Orange Lodges, from Ulster and other parts of Ireland, gather peacefully to commemorate 'Good King Billy's' victory on the banks of the Boyne.

THE DONEGAL CORRIDOR: THE SECOND WORLD WAR ON THE ATLANTIC COAST

At the beginning of the Second World War, Taoiseach Éamon de Valera declared that Ireland would remain neutral. The fledgling Irish state was announcing to the world that it was an independent sovereign country. This decision disappointed the British and American allies, as Ireland's geographical location, on the edge of Europe, was vital to protecting the north-western approaches to Great Britain from the Atlantic.

The Anglo-Irish Treaty of 1921, which established the Irish Free State and partitioned Ireland, included a clause that allowed the British continued use of three Irish ports for naval, aviation and storage purposes. The ports, which became known as the Treaty Ports, were Queenstown (today Cobh) in Cork Harbour, along with Bere Island in Co. Cork and Lough Swilly in Co. Donegal, both along the Atlantic coast. In the 1920s, the British were more than aware of the strategic importance of retaining a foothold on the western fringes of the British Isles. History had shown that Ireland was a possible springboard for an invasion of Great Britain: the Jacobites in 1689, the French in 1798 and the more recent experience of the First World War and German U-boat attacks along the Atlantic coast. From an Irish perspective, the Government of the new state did not have the resources, financial or military, to operate the necessary defences, so at the time the Treaty Ports arrangement suited both countries.

The Anglo-Irish Trade war of the 1930s led to strained relations between Britain and Ireland. However, in 1938 lengthy negotiations led to a resolution of the issues. Part of that resolution was the British withdrawal from the Treaty Ports. Neville Chamberlain, then British Prime Minister, and the British military recognised that the ports needed updating, which would be costly. At the time of the handover, only four ships were stationed in the ports. Chamberlain believed that if a conflict broke out Ireland would take the British side and that the ports would once again be made available to the Royal Navy. Not everyone in London agreed with Chamberlain's decision. The Admiralty disagreed with the withdrawal, as did Winston Churchill, who thought it a 'feckless act'. He described the Treaty Ports as, 'the sentinel towers of the western approaches in the North Atlantic'. In April 1938, the Royal Navy left Cork and Donegal, which meant that it now had to defend the North Atlantic from 200 miles further east.

When the Second World War broke out on 3 September 1939, with no British presence in Ireland, de Valera was able to declare that the country would remain neutral. However, during what became known in Ireland as 'The Emergency', staying neutral became a challenge for de Valera and his Government.

Churchill's concern about the Atlantic was proved right when, within hours of the declaration of war, the first casualty was the passenger ship *Athenia*, travelling from Liverpool to

America, carrying 1,300 people, which was torpedoed by a German U-boat off the Co. Donegal coast. The submarine commander, Fritz Julius Lemp, thought he was firing on a naval ship. He offered no assistance to the sinking vessel and left the scene, later denying any involvement. These actions contravened the Hague Convention and were regarded as a war crime. The *Knute Nelson*, a Norwegian tanker, came to assist the stricken *Athenia*, and brought the survivors to Galway, the nearest neutral port. The first 112 casualties of the Second World War were British, Canadian and American civilians. The Battle of the Atlantic, the longest campaign of the war, had begun.

As the war progressed and European countries were invaded by Hitler, Britain found itself increasingly relying on North American imports of food and industrial raw material. To protect merchant ships against German submarine attacks, they travelled in convoy and under naval escort, and relied on air cover to hunt and bomb submarines. Thousands of merchant and naval ships and submarines were sunk between 1939 and the end of the war, with the loss of an estimated 60,000 Allied and German seamen.

Despite Ireland's neutrality, de Valera did lean in favour of the Allies. For example, Irish Coast Guards reported any sightings of German U-boats along the Atlantic Coast by sending uncoded messages out into the ether for anyone who cared to intercept them. German airmen who crash-landed in Ireland, perhaps due to shortage of fuel, were interned. However, British servicemen usually found themselves 'released' into Northern Ireland as they had 'accidentally' strayed into the Irish Free State on a training exercise.

On 2 February 1941, the first flight operated by Royal Air Force Coastal Command, flew out of Castle Archdale, a new base on the shores of Lough Erne, in Co. Fermanagh, the most westerly of the Northern Ireland counties. Royal Air Force and Royal Canadian Airforce Catalina and Sunderland flying boats carried out surveillance and bombing missions over the Atlantic, providing air cover over the 'Black Gap', an area of the Atlantic that previously could not be covered from bases on the British mainland.

However, valuable fuel and time were being wasted as, to avoid encroaching on the neutral air space of the Irish Free State, the aircraft had to travel north to Derry before veering west. A secret arrangement was made between the British and Irish governments allowing seaplanes from Castle Archdale to follow the course of the Erne river, over Belleek and across the border into Co. Donegal. They could fly over Ballyshannon and out over Donegal Bay, on condition that the aircraft remained at high altitude and that they did not go anywhere near Finner Camp, an Irish army base. This became known as 'the Donegal Corridor'. A reconnaissance aircraft that flew through the Donegal Corridor located the German battleship *Bismarck* in the North Atlantic in May 1941, which led to her sinking.

The Donegal Corridor was just one of the concessions that the Irish Government afforded the British and Allied Forces in what has been described as a 'benevolent neutrality', or what could also be called 'turning the blind eye'.

During the war, over 160 planes crashed or made forced landings along the Co. Donegal coastline, many of them having run out of fuel, as they tried to reach RAF Castle Archdale after an Atlantic mission. On 23 January 1944, a Halifax, carrying a crew of eight, on a meteorological surveillance mission, out of Tiree in Scotland, crashed into cliffs at Tullan Beach near Bundoran. Two women who worked at the nearby Great Northern Hotel went to help but the three RAF and five

Royal Canadian Air Force airmen all died in the crash. The bodies of two of the airmen were never recovered. However, not all crashes ended in tragedy. On 25 July 1942, two RAF pilots set off from Anglesey, North Wales, lost their bearings and, running low on fuel, landed their Westland Lysander on Ballyliffen Beach, on the Inishowen Peninsula. Both walked away unscathed. Locals provided them with food and shelter and the following day fuel for the plane was brought from Northern Ireland. In yet another concession to neutrality, the Irish Government allowed an armed tug boat, *Robert Hastie*, disguised as a fishing trawler and crewed by RAF personnel, to operate in Donegal Bay during the war as a search and rescue service for Allied planes.

The cessation of hostilities in 1945 brought an end to the familiar sight of military aircraft flying the Donegal Corridor.

GLENCOLUMCILLE: ST COLMCILLE

In western Scotland, one of the most revered saints from the early Christian period is St Columba, founder of a monastic settlement on the Hebridean island of Iona. From there he sent missionaries to convert the pagans of Scotland and the north of England to Christianity. He was, in fact, Irish and is better known as St Colmcille in his native Donegal, where his memory is kept alive with a pilgrimage each year in the Atlantic coastal valley that bears his name: Glencolmcille. However, this holy man left his beloved Donegal under a cloud of shame in AD 563.

St Colmcille was born at Gartan, in Donegal, in AD 521. Descended from a High King of Ireland, St Colmcille, which translates as 'Dove of the Church', trained as a scribe under St Finian of Movilla. Early Christian monasteries were places of learning, where monks produced the only books and were the only ones able to read them.

St Finian came into possession of a copy of St Jerome's Vulgate, which he intended translating into Gaelic. Unknown to him, St Colmcille borrowed the book and made a copy. On hearing about the copy, St Finian demanded that it, and the original, be returned to him. St Colmcille refused to surrender the copy and they referred their dispute to the highest authority in sixth-century Ireland, the High King. He judged that 'to every cow her calf, to every book, its copy' and St Colmcille was ordered to hand over the copied book. He did not agree with the verdict. The dispute escalated, with supporters and families of each saint eventually battling it out at Cúl Dreimhne on the slopes of Ben Bulben in Co. Sligo, in what became known as the 'Battle of the Books'. Feeling remorseful for the deaths of 3,000 souls in the battle, St Colmcille left Ireland, from Inishowen Head, in AD 563, crossing to Scotland intent on converting as many souls to Christianity as had died during the Battle of the Books. He was accompanied by twelve followers and they settled on Iona. He vowed never to lay eyes on his beloved Ireland again. He did return to Ireland once more, but wore a blindfold so as not to break his vow.

During his time in Scotland, he was walking one day along the shores of Loch Ness with a servant. He wanted to cross the loch but the boat he intended using had come adrift and was floating out of reach. St Colmcille ordered his servant to retrieve the boat and who obeyed by, plunging into the freezing water. Just as he reached the boat, the head of a monster was said to have broken through the surface, intent on devouring the terrified servant. St Colmcille, standing on the shoreline, remained calm and made the sign of the cross, while praying loudly. The monster took fright and retreated to the murky depths. The servant, though shaken, managed to recover himself and scramble into the boat. This is the first recorded sighting of the Loch Ness monster.

When St Colmcille died in AD 597, he was buried on Iona but it is said that centuries later his bones were brought to Downpatrick (today in Co. Down) to be buried alongside his fellow Irish saints, Patrick and Bridget, bringing the trinity of Ireland's three patron saints together.

To commemorate the centenary of his death, the monks on Iona began working on a commemorative masterpiece. Using swan quills, and inks they made themselves, they began transcribing the Four Gospels on vellum. In minute script, they decorated the edges of the pages with elaborate swirling patterns and zoomorphic images. With the threat of Viking attacks, the manuscript was moved to Kells in Co. Meath, a monastic site founded by St Colmcille, where it was completed. It is ironic that the Book of Kells, Ireland's most treasured book, is dedicated to the memory of St Colmcille, who had to leave Ireland because of an argument over another holy book.

GWEEDORE: MURDER, THE FIGHTING PRIEST OF GWEEDORE AND THE LAND WAR IN WEST DONEGAL

Between the villages of Milford and Carrigart, in west Donegal, a Celtic Cross monument, erected in 1960, commemorates three local men who were involved in a shooting at that spot on 2 April 1878. Unusually, the three men were the shooters and not the victims of the attack. The victim was Lord Leitrim, a local landlord, murdered at a time when tensions ran high between tenant and landlord, particularly in west Donegal.

By the late 1870s, little had changed in the western regions of Ireland since the Famine. Landlords still rented plots of land to tenant farmers, who struggled to make ends meet. Their tenure was not secure and they faced eviction at any time and for no reason. In the 1850s, John George Adair bought land at Glenveagh in Co. Donegal. He hoped to create a deer hunting park and farm sheep on his newly acquired land. To make way for the sheep, he evicted 244 tenants in 1861. A relief fund was set up in the county to assist those affected in emigrating to Australia.

Another landlord in the area was Lord Leitrim. William Sydney Clement inherited his Donegal estate in 1854 and also owned land in Kildare, Galway and Leitrim. He had a reputation as a heartless, bad-tempered landlord, and several assassination attempts were made on his life. He was convinced that he was being targeted by the liberal Lord Lieutenant of Ireland, Lord Carlisle, who did not approve of Leitrim's more conservative views. He should have looked closer to home.

A group of his tenants from the Fanad Peninsula plotted to assassinate him on the morning of 2 April 1878. Michael McElwee, Neil Shiel and Michael Heraghty lay in wait as Lord Leitrim left his home at Manorvaughan near Milford by carriage that morning. They each had a gun. When the carriage approached them, one shot killed the carriage driver, and another killed Leitrim's clerk, who was travelling with him. The third shot, aimed at Lord Leitrim, missed him and he fled. However, the assassins gave chase. Shiel caught him and bludgeoned him over the head with the butt of his gun. The three then fled the scene and rowed home across Mulroy Bay. While the murder of a landlord was shocking news, few mourned Lord Leitrim.

Nonetheless, justice had to be done. Investigations led the police to McElwee's door and that of two neighbours, Bernard and Thomas McGranahan. They were all arrested. The evidence against McElwee linked him to a fragment of a gun found at the scene. The McGranahans were arrested because a piece of paper, also found at the scene, and used as wadding in the gun, was traced back to a schoolbook belonging to their sister. After a year in prison, the case against them was dropped. McElwee died of typhus while awaiting trial. The man who actually murdered Lord Leitrim, Neil Shiel, was never charged and died in 1921.

In 1879 crop failure, rising prices and bad weather saw Ireland returning to near-famine conditions. The Irish National Land League, founded in Co. Mayo in 1879 by Michael Davitt and Charles Stewart Parnell, took up the cause of the tenant farmer and began a programme of agitation against the stranglehold of landlordism. Their long-term aim was for tenant farmers to own land. The Land War of 1879–82 saw the Land League organising relief to stave off famine, and agitation against landlords unwilling to reduce rents. The champions of the tenants and supporters of the Land League were often the Catholic parish priests. They encouraged tenants to withhold rent from landlords who refused to comply with the Land League's requests, even though the organisation had been outlawed in 1881. Fr James McFadden was one such priest, who became known as 'the fighting priest of Gweedore'.

Fr McFadden was born in Carrigart in 1842, during the Famine year. With one uncle an Archbishop and another a Cardinal, his career into the priesthood was predetermined from a young age. He attended the seminary in Maynooth and was ordained in 1871. By 1875, Fr McFadden was the parish priest in Gweedore. He had a reputation as a strict disciplinarian, regularly bursting into shebeens, where illegal poteen was being served, and threatening the revellers by brandishing his blackthorn stick. In fact, he seemed to frown on any kind of revelry, as he also broke up evenings of dancing and music. He once found a group of children listening at the door of a house where adults were enjoying the music of a local piper. Not only did he break up the gathering, but all in attendance were denounced from the altar the following Sunday, and the children were to attend Mass daily for the next week, walking to the church barefoot. It was the month of February.

Despite his religious zeal, he came to be known as 'An Sagart Mór' or the 'Big Priest', not because of his stature but because he championed local tenant farmers in their perpetual struggles with landlords. This often landed him in serious trouble.

In 1888, Fr McFadden spent three months in prison for blocking bailiffs from entering a cottage to carry out the eviction of some tenants in his parish. On his release, he continued to impede evictions. On 3 February, he was saying Sunday mass at Derrybeg church when the church was stormed by members of the Royal Irish Constabulary, led by District Inspector William Martin. They were there to arrest Fr McFadden for once again obstructing an eviction of parishioners, earlier that week. Perhaps it was not wise to attempt the arrest with such a supportive crowd present. A scuffle broke out and Martin fell over, hitting his head. He died from his injuries, deemed to have been murdered. Fr McFadden and thirty parishioners were rounded up and charged with the crime. The trial was held, not in Donegal, but in Maryborough (now Portlaoise), 300km away, as the Attorney General knew that he could not get a Donegal jury to convict a priest. One hundred and fifty of Fr McFadden's parishioners travelled to Maryborough for the trial to support him and the twelve other Donegal men being tried. In the end, the State agreed to drop the case if all those being charged pleaded guilty, and between them the twelve men served a thirty-year prison sentence. Fr McFadden was released. He returned to Donegal and was moved to the parish of Glenties. The Land Acts of the late nineteenth century brought some resolution to the land problems of Ireland and Fr McFadden spent the last years of his ministry breaking up jovial gatherings. He died in 1917.

THE BATTLE OF TORY: THE ONLY SEA BATTLE ON THE ATLANTIC COAST

No historical journey of a coastline would be complete without a story of a sea battle. The engagement between the British and French navies off the Co. Donegal coast on 12 October 1798, the Battle of Tory (sometimes called the Battle of Donegal) was the last engagement by the French in their efforts to help the United Irishmen overthrow British rule in Ireland. On board one of the French vessels was Theobald Wolfe Tone, a leading member of the United Irishmen.

In 1796, he had successfully persuaded the French to invade Ireland and join the efforts of the United Irishmen in establishing an Irish republic. However, that expedition to Bantry Bay, in December 1796, failed due to the notorious Irish weather. By 1798 Napoleon Bonaparte was ruling France and Wolfe Tone petitioned him for another French force to invade Ireland. Meanwhile, in Ireland, the United Irishmen were outlawed and those suspected of membership were being rounded up. The floggings, punishments and reign of terror led to a brief uprising in Co. Wexford.

Napoleon sent 1,100 French soldiers and three French ships to Ireland in August 1798. Led by General Humbert, they came ashore at Kilcummin Beach on Killala Bay, Co. Mayo. They quickly took control of Ballina and marched on Castlebar, surprising the English garrison, who fled. This event became known as 'the Races of Castlebar'. However, the Irish who joined the fray were inexperienced soldiers. General Humbert knew the fight was futile and on 8 September 1798, at Ballinamuck, Co. Longford, he surrendered. The French soldiers were treated as prisoners of war but the Irish who had fought alongside them were executed.

Just over a week later, on 16 September, Wolfe Tone was once again sailing from France to Ireland, this time on board *Hoche*. The fleet, under Admiral Jean-Baptiste Bompart, was made up of just ten ships. Unaware of General Humbert's surrender, they were sailing into certain failure. Adding to their woes, the Royal Navy was on high alert after General Humbert's landing at Killala. They were watching any French naval activity in the English Channel, and as soon as the fleet carrying Wolfe Tone put to sea they were spotted and pursued. In a bid to shake off the Royal Navy, Bompart veered west, as if heading for America. However, HMS *Amelia* continued to follow. Eventually Bompart had to give up any pretence, and veered north-east, giving away his true destination as Ireland. A faster brig was sent to warn Sir John Borlase Warren, Commander of the Irish station of the Royal Navy.

The French managed to stay ahead of their British chasers and took shelter off Tory Island. On the morning of 11 October, the French saw sails on the horizon. The weather was changing and with the Royal Navy so close, the plan to land in Ireland was abandoned. The French fleet headed out to sea, hoping to avoid the Royal Navy and return to France. But they headed straight into a storm, which took its toll on *Hoche*. Badly damaged, and unable to outrun the Royal Navy, the only option open to Bompart was to make a stand. The scene was set for the only sea battle on Ireland's Atlantic coast. The first shots were fired at seven o'clock on the morning of 12 October 1798. *Hoche* became isolated from her protecting fleet and surrendered at eleven o'clock. The Battle of Tory was over. Wolfe Tone, the only Irishman on board, had operated a gun during the battle. The fleet was escorted into Lough Swilly and as the prisoners were disembarking at Buncrana, Wolfe Tone was immediately recognised and put in fetters. A known leader of the United Irishmen, he was a wanted man. He was brought to Dublin, where he was tried for treason. At his sentencing, he pleaded for a soldier's death by firing squad but was sentenced to be hanged. He attempted suicide on 10 November and died of his wounds nine days later.

The Battle of Tory was the last engagement of the 1798 Rebellion. The rebellion was defeated and the British had once again confirmed their naval dominance over the French. Napoleon's attempt to invade the British Isles had ended in failure, and the French would offer no future assistance to further the cause of Irish republicanism. Three of Bompart's fleet limped back to France and the remaining seven ships were captured and put into service with the Royal Navy. *Hoche* was renamed and seven years later served in the Battle of Trafalgar as HMS *Donegal*.

FLIGHT OF THE EARLS

This historic journey along Ireland's Atlantic coast began with the Battle of Kinsale, fought in December 1601. It brought to an end the Nine Years' War', waged by the Gaelic lords of Ulster, Red Hugh O'Donnell, and Hugh O'Neill, Earl of Tyrone, against the English forces of Elizabeth I. Had the

Spaniards who came to their assistance arrived on the coast of the O'Donnell stronghold in Donegal and not at the other end of the Wild Atlantic Way perhaps the history of Ireland would have been different.

Who were these troublesome Ulster lords and what were their fates after the Battle of Kinsale?

Hugh O'Neill's grandfather pledged allegiance to Henry VIII, in 1541, earning him the English title Earl of Tyrone. Under the English law of primogeniture, Matthew, his eldest son, was next in succession. Hugh's brother, Shane, had other ideas. In a power grab, he killed Matthew and for good measure exiled Mathew's son and heir, Hugh O'Neill. Hugh grew up in the Pale, the most anglicised part of Ireland, where he was educated in the English way. He joined the English army, fighting against the Munster lords during the Desmond rebellion. He returned to Ulster, and with the support of the Crown, recovered family lands and reclaimed the Earldom of Tyrone in 1587. Hugh O'Neill portrayed all the signs of being a loyal English subject.

Meanwhile, on the Atlantic seaboard of Ulster, towards the end of the 1580s, Hugh McManus O'Donnell of Tyrconnell, in Donegal, was not the model English lord: far from it. He was rooted in his Gaelic ways. When his 15-year-old son, Red Hugh O'Donnell, was betrothed to Rose O'Neill, daughter of the Earl of Tyrone, Lord Deputy Perrot, the Queen's representative in Ireland, believed that an alliance of the O'Donnell and O'Neill clans could only spell trouble.

A common practice in Elizabethan times was to kidnap and hold hostage the sons of troublesome lords. As long as the family did not create trouble, the son would be safe. In 1587, Lord Deputy Perrot devised a plan to kidnap Red Hugh O'Donnell. His spies informed him that Red Hugh was at Rathmelton, staying at an abbey, on the shores of Lough

Swilly. A ship from Dublin docked on the quayside and the unsavoury crew put it about that they had wine for sale. Red Hugh was lured on board under the pretext of sampling some of the fine wine. He sampled enough not to notice that the ship had set sail and that he was now on his way to Dublin, more specifically, Dublin Castle, where he was held captive. He made a dramatic escape but he was too weak for the arduous trek over the Dublin Mountains. He sought refuge with the O'Toole clan, who handed him back to the authorities at Dublin Castle. He lost two toes to frostbite in the process and was thereafter kept manacled to prevent another escape attempt. But Red Hugh was determined to return to Donegal and on Christmas Day 1592, along with two of the O'Neills also in captivity, he escaped through the sewers of Dublin Castle. Later that year, Red Hugh succeeded his father as the chief of the O'Donnells.

In Ulster, Hugh O'Neill had gone rogue. He saw Protestant settlers coming into parts of Ulster, saw English sheriffs taking control of governance and he did not like it. His absence from the Royal Court was soon noted and before long the model English lord had aligned himself with that most Gaelic of clans, the O'Donnells, and was poised for rebellion. Their common goal was to keep Ulster Gaelic and Catholic. This led to the Nine Years' War', which ended with their defeat at the Battle of Kinsale in 1601.

In the immediate aftermath of Kinsale, Red Hugh O'Donnell boarded a ship at Castlehaven, in West Cork, bound for Spain. His purpose was to seek an audience with King Phillip III and persuade him to send more ships to Ireland, to further the Catholic cause. In September 1602 he was on his way to Valladolid for that audience when he dropped dead at Simancas. An English spy, working for Lord Deputy Mountjoy, is thought to have poisoned him. That is a far more heroic death than the version that suggests he died from tapeworm. His titles, lands and his cause were taken up by his son, Rory.

With the death of Red Hugh O'Donnell, and realising that no further help would be coming from Spain, Hugh O'Neill reached a settlement with the English. He signed the Treaty of Mellifont in March 1603, the conditions of which required him and Rory O'Donnell to abandon the Gaelic Brehon law in favour of English law, to use the English language and to pledge allegiance to the Crown. On signing the document, O'Neill thought he was pledging allegiance to Queen Elizabeth. Mountjoy failed to tell him that the Queen had died some days earlier. The new monarch, the Scottish King James I, was lenient towards O'Neill, who had fought for the Scots in the past. He and Rory O'Donnell visited London, pledged their allegiance, and were granted lands in Tyrone and Tyrconnell respectively. O'Donnell even came away with an English title after King James I created him 1st Earl Tyrconnell.

However, neither earl was happy with the changes brought to their lives. Their power and old way of life was gone and by 1607 they had decided to leave Ireland. In September 1607, the Earls of Tyrone and Tyrconnell, with ninety-seven members of their families, boarded a ship at Rathmullan, on Lough Swilly. The Flight of the Earls was under way. One of O'Neill's sons was accidentally left behind in the confusion. They landed at Quillebof at the mouth of the Seine in France. They wintered in Spanish Flanders, still hopeful of making their way to Spain and securing help from Philip III in raising an army. Philip III had, however, made peace with the new English king and could no longer offer help or succour. In the spring of 1608, the Earls made their way to Rome and came under the protection of the Pope. Rory, Earl of Tyrconnell, died there in 1608 and is buried in the church of St Piedro Montario. Hugh O'Neill, Earl of Tyrone, remained in Rome, never to return to Ireland, and died there in 1616. With the Flight of the Earls any hope of reviving Gaelic Catholic Ireland was lost.

History is the gift that keeps on giving. An archaeological dig at Valladolid in Spain in 2020 revealed a skeleton thought to be that of Red Hugh O'Donnell. Unfortunately, as the skeleton had all ten toes, and it was a known fact that Red Hugh had lost two of his to frostbite, the search continues for his last resting place.

BUNCRANA: THE AMAZING GRACE CONNECTION

The popular hymn 'Amazing Grace' was composed in the eighteenth century by the slave trader John Newton following a life-changing experience that brought him to the shores of Buncrana. Perhaps the most famous hymn of all time, it is still sung in churches across all Christian faiths today and has been recorded by Elvis and Johnny Cash, among others.

Newton was born in London in 1725. His father was a merchant mariner and took his son to sea when he was just 11. He worked his way from cabin boy to midshipman but had a reputation for being difficult. His language would have made a sailor blush and he did not believe in God. He was press-ganged into the Royal Navy, rebelled at the conditions, and deserted, only to be captured and flogged. Because he was so troublesome, the Navy wanted to be rid of him and he was sent to work on the slave ship *Orange*. On board, Newton's fiery temperament so infuriated the captain that he abandoned him on the west coast of Africa. There he himself was forced into slavery, working for an English slave trader. Newton's father had grown concerned for his son's safety and asked the captain of *The Greyhound* to search for him at ports in West Africa. He found Newton, still an angry atheist, and took him on board as a passenger bound for Liverpool in late March 1748. During that voyage, the ship encountered a violent storm. Crew members were blown overboard, while the creaking wooden ship was tossed on the high seas. In his terror, Newton found himself begging God to spare him. The ship limped into Lough Swilly and docked at Buncrana on 8 April 1748, where the passengers disembarked. Here, Newton wrote the first verse of 'Amazing Grace'. God had answered his prayer and had saved 'a wretch' like him. As he stepped on to dry land at Buncrana, he believed that God had shown mercy by saving his life and also his soul.

It was not a complete 'road to Damascus' conversion, however. Newton returned to Liverpool and became a captain on ships that operated the Slave Triangle between England, Africa and the West Indies. Even when he suffered a stroke and could no longer captain a ship he continued to invest in the slave trade.

After many years of Bible reading and study, he was allowed to take holy orders and was given a parish in Kent. He renounced slavery in 1788, writing a pamphlet entitled *Thoughts Upon the Slave Trade*, which he sent to every Member of Parliament in the run-up to the unsuccessful Abolition of Slavery Bill. In it, he described himself as 'a slaver who saw the light'. Newton later mentored William Wilberforce in his bid to abolish the slave trade, which was finally achieved in 1807 by the Trans-Atlantic Slave Trade Act. John Newton died in 1807 but lived just long enough to know that his life's work was complete.

LOUGH SWILLY:
THE FIRST WORLD WAR

Sheltered by the Fanad Peninsula and the Inishowen Peninsula, the deep waters of Lough Swilly have, for centuries, provided a safe haven for ships. During the First World War, Lough Swilly was to see more shipping activity than ever before as it became a strategic shelter for naval and merchant shipping activity in the North Atlantic.

On 22 October 1914, three months into the war, people living on the shores of Lough Swilly watched as the Grand Fleet of the Royal Navy steamed its way into the lough, where, for the next month, forty battleships, minesweepers and tankers were temporarily taking shelter. It was a magnificent sight but brought the reality of war to the shores of Donegal.

Ordinarily stationed at Scapa Flow in the Orkney Islands, Commander of the Fleet Admiral Jellicoe had ordered that the Grand Fleet be dispersed between Loch Ewe, on the west coast of Scotland, and Lough Swilly while the defences at Scapa Flow were being updated. The submarine was the new weapon of war and the German Navy intended using it to disrupt trade routes and British naval activity in the North Atlantic and the North Sea. Undetected underwater, their U-boats could torpedo ships, or lay minefields in shipping lanes, causing major disruption and casualties. They could also sneak into deep harbours and attack anchored ships, hence the need to update the defences at Scapa Flow.

At Lough Swilly, a boom was erected between Macamish Point, on the west shore of Lough Swilly, and Ned's Point on the east, to protect the harbour and the anchored fleet. This would remain in place for the duration of the war.

While assured that a U-boat could not enter Lough Swilly, the damage they could cause at sea became a reality on 26 October 1914 when the SS *Manchester Commerce*, a cargo steamship en route from Manchester to Montreal, ran into a minefield laid by a German U-boat 32 km off Tory Island. Fourteen of the forty-four crew perished. News of this tragedy did not reach the Admiralty in time to prevent them sending a convoy of six ships out of Lough Swilly the following day on gunnery practice. They had no reason to suspect that the Germans could have laid a minefield that far west. At 8.45 a.m., HMS *Audacious* entered the same minefield and struck one. The ocean liner, *Olympic,* the sister ship of *Titanic,* was passing the scene at the time and tried to tow her to safety. Heavy seas and a snapped tow line led to the decision for all crew to abandon ship. All were saved, but HMS *Audacious* sank. The War Office and Admiral Jellicoe felt that news of such a loss would be bad for naval and public morale. They also did not want Germany to know that they had successfully sunk a Royal Naval vessel, so news of the sinking was kept from the press. Photographs taken by passengers on board *Olympic* were confiscated and, to further the ruse, another ship served throughout the war as HMS *Audacious*. It was 1919 before the public was officially told of the sinking.

Lough Swilly waved the Grand Fleet off in November 1914, but throughout the war, various naval ships came and went. It also became a rendezvous point for merchant ships, which travelled in convoy across the Atlantic.

As the war progressed, the dangers came nearer and in 1917 HMS *Laurentic* sank at the mouth of Lough Swilly, off Dunree Head, after striking a mine. The ship was carrying gold bullion when she sank. *Laurentic*'s story began in the Harland and Wolff dockyard in Belfast, where she was launched in 1908. As a White Star Line vessel, SS *Laurentic* operated as a luxury liner between Liverpool and ports in North America. She gained some fame as a passenger ship in 1910 having played a part in the capture of the fugitive Hawley Crippen, an American doctor who had murdered his wife. Scotland Yard suspected him of the crime when they found part of his wife's dismembered body in their home after he had fled to Europe. On a sailing of the passenger ship SS *Montrose* from Antwerp to Canada, the captain recognised the fugitive among his first-class passengers and, using the latest wireless telegraphy equipment, wired London. Scotland Yard's Detective Walter Dew boarded *Laurentic*, the next available ship crossing the Atlantic, which, as a much faster ship, reached Canada before *Montrose*. In the St Lawrence river, Detective Dew boarded *Montrose* disguised as a pilot and was able to arrest Dr Crippen. He was found guilty of murder and was hanged in Pentonville Prison later that year.

When the First World War broke out, the ship was commandeered by the Royal Navy for use as an armed auxiliary cruiser. On 23 January 1917, *Laurentic* set sail from Liverpool to Halifax in Nova Scotia on a top-secret mission. Along with a crew of 475, in her cargo hold were 3,211 gold bars, worth £5 million (approximately £300 million today).

The gold bullion was payment for munitions the British Government had bought in Canada and America.

Shortly after leaving Liverpool, five sailors became ill, displaying signs of yellow fever. Captain Norton made the decision to sail into Lough Swilly for an unscheduled port of call at Buncrana to put the sick sailors ashore. The officers took the opportunity to take shore leave and dined that evening in the Swilly Hotel.

On the morning of 25 January, a snowstorm and gale-force winds were battering the north and west coasts of Ireland. Nonetheless, *Laurentic* headed for sea. Forty-five minutes after leaving Buncrana, between Fanad Head and Dunree Head, the ship entered a recently laid German minefield, where she struck two mines and sank within an hour. Weather conditions prevented rescue ships from assisting. While lifeboats were successfully launched from *Laurentic,* weather conditions meant that of the 475 people on board, 354 perished. Lifeboats were found afterwards with the oars frozen to the hands of the dead sailors. In later weeks bodies were washed up as far away as the Outer Hebrides.

At the bottom of the ocean, along with those sailors who met their end without escaping *Laurentic,* was the gold bullion. Recovery of the gold was essential and so the top divers of the

Royal Navy were assigned the task. After weeks of diving, they eventually managed to break into the safe holding the gold. Using basic diving equipment, bringing the cumbersome crates of gold to the surface was dangerous. Bad weather interrupted the progress, with one particular storm sending the gold deeper into the wreck. By September 1917, the war was entering a critical phase and it was decided that recovering the rest of the gold was no longer a priority. If the best naval divers could not easily retrieve the gold, no one else could and it would be there after the war. The bulk of the gold was brought to the surface in 1919, with only twenty-five bars unaccounted for. In the 1930s, a further three bars were recovered. It is, therefore, possible that gold treasure is still hidden in the now scattered wreckage of the *Laurentic*.

By coincidence, a later White Star ship called SS *Laurentic*, built at Harland and Wolfe, Belfast, in 1927, was torpedoed off the Co. Donegal coast near Bloody Foreland, on 3 November 1940, a casualty of the Second World War.

BIBLIOGRAPHY

Arrowsmith, Aidan (Ed.), *The Complete Works of J.M. Synge Plays, Prose and Poetry* (Wordsworth Poetry Library, 2008).

Bardon, Jonathan, *A History of Ireland in 250 Episodes* (Gill Books, 2008).

Bench-Jones, Mark, *Life in an Irish Country House* (Constable and Company, 1996).

Brown, Terence, *The Life of W.B. Yeats* (Gill and Macmillan, 2001).

Burke, Ray, *Joyce County* (Currach Press, 2016).

Connolly, S.J. (Ed.), *The Oxford Companion to Irish History* (Oxford University Press, 1998).

Coogan, Tim Pat, *De Valera Long Fellow, Long Shadow* (Hutchinson, 1993).

Coogan, Tim Pat, *Michael Collins* (Arrow Books, 1991).

Cowell, John, *Sligo Land of Yeats Desire* (O'Brien Press, 1990).

Doherty, Neal, *The Statues and Sculptures of Dublin City* (Orpen Press, 2015).

Ekin, Des, *The Stolen Village: Baltimore and the Barbary Pirates* (O'Brien Press Ltd, 2008).

Hegarthy, Shane, O'Toole, Fintan, *The Irish Times Book of the 1916 Rising* (Gill and Macmillan, 2006).

Fallon, Niall, *The Armada in Ireland* (Stanford Maritime Ltd, 1978).

Eoghan, Patrick, *Daniel O'Connell: The Man Who Discovered Ireland* (Glasnevin Trust, 2010).

James, Dermott, *The Gore Booths of Lissadell* (The Woodfield Press, 2004).

Keane, Elizabeth, *Seán MacBride: A Life* (Gill and Macmillan, 2007).

Kee, Robert, *The Green Flag Volume I The Most Distressful Country* (Penguin Books, 1972).

Kee, Robert, *The Green Flag Volume II The Bold Fenian Men* (Penguin Books, 1972).

Kee Robert, *The Green Flag Volume III Ourselves Alone* (Penguin Books, 1972).

Kinsella, Thomas, *The Táin Translated* (Oxford University Press, 1969).

Knatchbull, Timothy, *From a Clear Blue Sky* (Arrow, 2010).

Laffan, William (Ed.), *The Cliffs of Moher and the O'Brien Legacy* (The Follies Trust, 2018).

Litton, Helen (Ed.), *Revolutionary Woman Kathleen Clarke: An Autobiography* (O'Brien Press, 1991).

Lysaght, Charles (Ed.), *Great Irish Lives* (HarperCollins Publishers, 2008).

McGowan, Joe (Ed.), *Constance Markievicz* (Consatance Markievicz Millenium Committee, 2003).

MacLaughlin, Jim (Ed.), *Donegal: The Making of a Nation County* (Four Courts Press, 2007).

MacThomáis, Shane, *Glasnevin Ireland's Necropolis* (Glasnevin Trust, 2010).

Marquess of Sligo, *Westport House and the Brownes* (Moorland Publishing Co. Ltd, 1981).

Moody, T.W, Martin, F.X. (Eds), *The Course of Irish History* (Mercier Press, 1967).

Morgan, Hiram, *The Battle of Kinsale* (Wordwell Books, 2004).

Murphy, Fr Ignatius, *Fr Michael Meehan and the Ark of Kilbaha* (St Flannans [Killaloe] Diocesan Trust).

Nancollas, Tom, *Seashaken Houses, A Lighthouse History from Eddystone to Fastnet* (Penguin Books, 2019).

O'Brien, Jacqueline Harbison, Peter, *Ancient Ireland from Prehistory to the Middle Ages* (Weidenfeld & Nicholson, 1996).

O'Callaghan, Tony, *The Kerry Coast* (Tony O'Callaghan, 2016).

O'Connor, Ulick, *Celtic Dawn: A Portrait of the Irish Literary Renaissance* (Town House and Country House, 1999).

O'Hara, Bernard, *Exploring Mayo* (Killasser/Callow Heritage Society, 2017).

O'Reilly, Roger, *Lighthouses of Ireland* (The Collins Press, 2018).

Spellissy, Séan, *The History of Galway City and County* (Celtic Bookshop, 1999).

Thuillier, J., *History of Kinsale* (J.R. Thullier, 2001).

Wilkins, Noel P., *Alexander Nimmo Master Engineer 1783–1832* (Irish Academic Press, 2009).

Woodham-Smith, Cecil, *The Great Hunger* (Hamish Hamilton, 1962).

JOURNALS, MAGAZINES AND NEWSPAPERS

Bunbury, Turtle, 'Lord Sligo's Plunder of Ancient Greece' (*History Ireland*, Vol. 22 No. 3, May/June 2014).

Carroll, Francis M., 'The First Casualty of the Sea: The Athenia Survivors and the Galway Relief Effort, Sept 1939' (*History Ireland*, Vol. 19 No. 1, Jan/Feb 2011).

Chambers, Anne, 'Champion of Slaves-Howe Peter Browne, 2nd Marquess of Sligo (1788–1845)' (*History Ireland*, No. 1 Vol. 26, Jan/Feb 2018).

Collins, Timothy, 'The Galway Line in Context: A Contribution to Galway Maritime History' (*Galway Archeological and Historical Society*, Vol. 46, 1994).

Connell Joseph E.A., 'Jeremiah O'Donovan Rossa's Funeral' (*History Ireland*, Vol. 23 No. 4, July/Aug 2015).

Guthrie, R., *HMS Laurentic* (*North Irish Roots*, Vol. 13 No. 1, 2002).

Kinsella, A., 'John Francis O'Reilly: The "Flighty Boy"' (*History Ireland*, Vol. 14 No. 1, Jan/Feb 2006).

McIntyre, Perry, 'Cornelius O'Brien and the Cliffs of Moher' (Vol. 15 No. 1 Mar/Apr 2007).

McGarry, Stephen, 'The French Fleet at Bantry Bay 1796' (*History Ireland*, Vol. 24 No. 6, Nov/Dec 2016).

McGowan, J., 'The Donegal Corridor and the Battle of the Atlantic' (*History Ireland*, Vol. 11 No. 2, Summer 2003).

McGurk, John, 'The Battle of Kinsale' (*History Ireland*, Vol. 9 No. 3, Autumn 2001).

Mitchell, James, 'The Rescue of Passengers and Crew of the Connaught, October 7 1860' (*Galway Archeological and Historical Society*, Vol. 63, 2011).

Morgan, Hiram, 'Gaelic Lordship and Tudor Conquest: Tír Eoghain, 1541–1603' (*History Ireland*, Vol. 13 No. 2, Sept/Oct 2005).

Moran, Gerard, 'James Hack Tuke and His Schemes for Assisted Emigration from the West of Ireland' (*History Ireland*, Vol. 21 No. 3, May/June 2013).

Murphy, Damien, 'Blacksod Point Lighthouse, Co. Mayo' (*History Ireland*, Vol. 23 No. 2, March/April 2015).

Murray, Theresa D., 'From Baltimore to Barbary: The 1631 Sack of Baltimore' (*History Ireland*, Vol. 14 No. 4, Jul/Aug 2006).

O'Loughlin, Joe, 'The Donegal Corridor during the Second World

War' (*Clogher Record*, Vol. 18 No. 2, 2004).

O'Loughlin, Thomas, 'St Patrick: The Legend and the Bishop' (*History Ireland*, Vol. 14 No. 1, Jan/Feb 2006).

O'Sullivan, Muiris, Downey, Liam, 'Martello and Signal Towers' (*Archeology Ireland*, Summer 2012).

Royle, Stephen, 'Leaving the Dreadful Rocks' (*History Ireland*, Vol. 7 No. 2, Summer 1999).

Tiernan, Sonja, 'In Defence of Barmaids: The Gore Booth Sisters Take on Winston Churchill' (*History Ireland*, Vol. 20 No. 3, May/June 2012).

Walker, Brian M., 'Southern Orange Commemorations, Past and Present' (*History Ireland*, Vol. 20 No. 5, Sept/Oct 2012).

Warner, Guy, 'The Flying Boats of Foynes' (*History Ireland*, Vol. 9 No. 1, Spring 2001).

Archeology Ireland Heritage Guide No. 79, The Spanish Armada Wrecks, Streedagh, Co. Sligo.

Journal of Cork Historical and Archeological Society, Jan/Dec 1990.

Journal of Cork Historical and Archeological Society, Vol. 74 July/ Dec 1996.

WEBSITES

www.clarelibrary.ie
www.diving.ie
www.igs.ie
www.irishlights.ie
www.lookoutposts.com
www.mayolibrary.ie
www.militaryarchives.ie
www.ww2irishaviation.com

ABOUT THE AUTHOR

Helen Lee has worked as a tour guide throughout Ireland and Great Britain since 1994. She has been a Fáilte Ireland-approved tour guide for Galway since 2004 and is the author of *The Little Book of Galway*.

ACKNOWLEDGEMENTS

I would like to thank Barbara McCarthy for reading early drafts, Paul Lee and Franco De Bonis for proof reading and my 'book club' girls for all their encouragement during the writing of this book. Special thanks to Geraldine, Franco and Theo for their endless support. Illustrations of Corcomroe Abbey and the Blasket Islands in Chapter 1 were drawn by my late uncle, Christy Munroe. Thank you to Eileen Munroe for letting me use them. All other illustrations are my own.